The Righteous Are Bold

A Play in Three Acts

by Frank Carney

A Samuel French Acting Edition

SAMUEL FRENCH

FOUNDED 1830

SAMUELFRENCH.COM

THE RIGHTEOUS ARE BOLD

(6 males; 4 females)

STORY OF THE PLAY

Author Frank Carney is concerned with such fundamental ideas as reason vs. faith, and superstition vs. religion. His script has to do with a girl who returns to the poor farmhouse in which she was born in Ireland's County Mayo, after working in England during World War II. It is obvious that she is emotionally disturbed. A well-meaning doctor, who seeks to find a reason behind everything, thinks her condition can be bettered in a hospital. But the family priest is certain that she is the victim of evil spirits as a result of having been used as a spiritualist's contact. There is an eerie and fascinating climactic scene in which the devout Father, through belief, exorcises the demons from the haunted girl. It is a tense and gripping episode. It appeared to bring the firstnighters forward to the edges of their seats. *The Righteous Are Bold* boasts folk writing that is evocative. It has a goodly measure of merit.

THE RIGHTEOUS ARE BOLD

Play by Frank Carney; staged by Eddie Dowling; setting by Watson Barratt; lighting by Peggy Clark; costumes by Audre; presented by Mr. Dowling at the Holiday Theatre, December 22, 1955. The cast:

MARY KATE GERATY .... *Nora O'Mahoney*
MICHAEL MARTIN GERATY .... *Len Doyle*
WILLIE THE POST .... *P. J. Kelly*
ANTHONY COSTELLO .... *Liam Gannon*
PATRICK GERATY .... *James Neylin*
NORA GERATY .... *Irene Hayes*
DR. MORAN .... *Bryan Herbert*
FATHER O'MALLEY .... *Denis O'Dea*
MOTHER BENEDICT .... *Frederica Going*
SISTER MARY OF THE ROSARY ... *Mary O'Brady*

The Scene is the same throughout. It is the kitchen of a poor farmhouse on the western ridge of Croagh Patrick in the County of Mayo in Ireland.

The time is 1945.

The Righteous Are Bold

ACT ONE

*The scene is the kitchen of a poor farmhouse built into the
rocks of Taobh na Cruaiche, the Western ridge of
Croagh Patrick, a holy mountain in County Mayo.
The house has the appearance of being swept bare and
clean by the high winds of Heaven. Behind is the
central cone of the mountain with a simple oratory
on its peak. Towards the South is the endless brown
moorland of North Connemara—wild savage desolate
moorland—veined with bog rivers and streaked with
lonesome, white roads. Towards the North, Clew Bay
—a glittering lace of inland waters and countless
islands. To the West, again the dreary turflands, the
grey clutter of houses in the small town of Louisburg
and the surging, white edge of the coast. Beyond that
is the Atlantic Ocean, deep, green-black water, white-
topped mountains of waves, danger and unknown
things. (See ground plan back of book.)*

*In this altitude the whitewash of the kitchen is
brilliant. A large rock can be seen through the door
at the back and the rocks into which the house is built
jut out here and there from the base of the walls and
form a crude hearthstone for the open fireplace. In
the fireplace are hobs and an iron crane. On a black
dresser hang lustre ware bought many years ago in
the distant town of Westport, old yellow jugs and
delph and large cracked plates with a willow pattern.
To one side of the door is the cailleach with curtains
and pelmet of paisley design. In the cailleach is a
high feather bed covered with a patchwork quilt.*

5

*There is an old black settle. There are sugan chairs
and a scrubbed, deal table. The floor is of slabs of
stone, worn smooth. A small, square, four-paned window has a blind and lace curtains. Harness hangs on
the walls at the side. A coloured, plaster statue of
Our Lady of the Immaculate Conception has a lamp
in front of it. The statue stands on a small wooden
shelf. Also hanging are a holy-water font, a picture
of the Sacred Heart and old, cheap calendars adver-
tising traders in the towns of Louisburg and Westport.
A door leads to the Left; another to the Right.
Through the window and back door can be seen
stones dangling from sugan ropes which are there to
keep the thatch secure against the sudden squalls
that sweep down from the mountain. Seagulls are
heard and a whistling wind. The house is high up on
the side of the mountain and the air is clear.*

AT RISE: *When the Curtain rises the stage is empty.* MARY
KATE GERATY *is heard off. She is shouting at an ani-
mal:* "Go on. Go on outa that. Dhursh. Dhursh. On
outa that with you." *She enters, carrying a stick
which she throws in a corner. In a pre-occupied manner, she goes to an immense pot in which stands a
wooden pounder. She pounds the contents for a moment, carries the pot to the fire and hangs it on the
crane. She is about fifty years of age and is worn
thin with fighting against nature in this wild country.
Her husband has by now crossed by the door, carrying a rock. Through the window we can see him tying
it to a rope which hangs from the thatch. He is of the
same age as his wife and is a wild, mountainy man.*

MARY. *(Crossing to door)* If you're finished hanging
them stones on the roof you might bring me a brestle of
turf.

(After a moment MICHAEL MARTIN *disappears.* MARY
KATE *goes to the cabinet and takes down an opened*

letter which she removes from the envelope and ex-
amines in an illiterate way. As her husband enters
with an armwul of turf she returns the letter to the
dresser.)

MICHAEL. There's mares' tails in the sky and white
horses out by Clare Island and I don't like that whistle in
the wind. *(Crosses to fireplace.)*

MARY. There'll be squalls blowing down from the mountain to-night. Have you them stones fixed tight on the
roof? *(Crosses up to door.)*

MICHAEL. I have faith. Saint Patrick drove the serpents
into the sea, but he left the winds of destruction behind.

(He is building the fire. MARY KATE *is at the door, look-*
ing up towards the mountain top.)

MARY. The windows in the chapel would dazzle you with
the sun on them. 'Tis a lonesome chapel I always think—
opening its doors to the pilgrims on one day only in the
year—and, for the rest, no company but the clouds that
sweep over the top of the mountain.

MICHAEL. Built strong against storm and wind—
(Building fire.)

MARY. You couldn't help feeling holy in the shelter of
it. *(She blesses herself with holy water from the font*
that hangs near the door.) Clew Bay is calm enough, God
knows. The islands to the East are like a lacey curtain
with the sun going down in the West and lighting up the
channels of water in between— There's hookers out from
Achill. Bringing turf to Westport I'd say.

MICHAEL. A dangerous life the sea.

MARY. There's plenty of money in fishing nowadays, all
the same.

MICHAEL. *(Stands up.)* I'd sooner the mountains any
day, rocks and stones and all. It's poor, hungry land but
I'm content.

MARY. Patrick is a long time up after the sheep. *(She*
gets letter from cabinet; crosses Left and gives it to him.)

I wonder how Nora is. Open up that letter again and read out to me what's in it.

MICHAEL. *(Crosses to table Left.)* What devil in hell drove her to England at all? Couldn't she settle down like others girls and Anthony Costello of Killsallagh full pelt after her to marry her?

MARY. *(Gets pot of potatoes from cabinet and starts paring them at table Left.)* People does daft things when they're young. We were young ourselves once.

MICHAEL. *(Standing alongside)* What's more, not writing for months and then a letter coming not from herself at all but from a priest. What, in the name of God, has a priest to do with it?

MARY. It mightn't have been easy getting someone to send word by.

MICHAEL. *(Gets specs from mantel and opens letter.)* On top it says "The Presbytery, Wallsham, near Bowden, Lancashire."

MARY. It's not the place she wrote from last.

MICHAEL. It might be where she was laid up— *(Sits down on hearth.)*

MARY. But the priest doesn't say what's wrong with her. Why doesn't he say? That's what's worrying me.

MICHAEL. *(Reading)* "Dear Mr. Geraty, I write to tell you that your daughter, Nora, has been well for some time is returning to Ireland shortly. She intends crossing as soon as her permit and sailing ticket are in order. I shall endeavour to let you know the date in advance. I am also writing by this post to her parish priest in Ireland who will, no doubt, see you in the matter. Yours faithfully in Jesus Christ, Quentin Richardson."

MARY. He'd be a priest, I suppose.

MICHAEL. Sure, what else would "in Jesus Christ" mean? *(Rises.)*

MARY. What did you say his name was?

MICHAEL. *(Stumbling over the name)* Quentin Richardson.

MARY. 'Tis a queer name for a priest. She must be the sick girl not to be able to write herself. Her brothers and sisters were never that long without writing and America is a deal further than England.

MIDHAEL. Whatever it is, I hope it isn't for want of keeping an eye on herself and going to the Sacraments regular. Father O'Malley is right—no human being should go to England at all.

MARY. That's no way for a father to talk about his own flesh and blood. If it was anything like that was the matter it wouldn't have stopped her writing this long.

MICHAEL. *(Throwing the letter on the table, crosses up; gazes at picture.)* The money they send is never worth the trouble and worry they leave behind. *(He goes to the door and looks out to the West.)*

(MARY *puts letter in cabinet.)*

Eleven children we reared and all of them gone from us but one.

MARY. *(Crossing to fireplace)* With Nora back itself, maybe things will be different.

MICHAEL. I wonder— Faith, here's Willie the Post.

MARY. It couldn't be he'd have another letter for us.

MICHAEL. What else would take him up the mountain road? He'll be all on for knowing what was in the letter he brung yesterday.

MARY. What he doesn't know won't trouble him. So, if he has another letter don't attempt to open it till he's gone. The less people knows the better.

MICHAEL. If there isn't anything Willie doesn't know— Put them shoes out before he crosses the threshold.

(To keep evil away from the house, MICHAEL MARTIN places a pair of shoes outside the threshold with the toes pointing outwards. WILLIE THE POST appears at the door with a bicycle. He is about fifty years of age and combines with the duties of postman those of the local medicine man. He wears an old-fashioned tweed costume, a red blouse and a bright-green hat. Dark-green stockings show above his laced boots. An old, black cycling cap hangs from his shoulders and is tied with cross straps over his breast. He wears

steel rimmed spectacles and has hat-tailed hair. His little eyes peer through the glasses. He leaves his bicycle outside.)

WILLIE. *(At the door.)* God save all here.

MARY *and* MICHAEL. God save you kindly.

WILLIE. *(Indicating the shoes)* Now, what evil could the postman bring to the house? Tell me that, Michael Martin Geraty. *(As they do not reply.)* I hope it isn't any harm ye'd be wishing on Willie McDermott.

(MARY KATE *attends to the fire. There is a threat in* WILLIE'S *voice.)*

MICHAEL. Arrah, herself would put the old shoes out if it was Father O'Malley himself was coming to the house. Them shoes goes out for near everyone enters the door.

> (WILLIE *comes into the kitchen, stepping gingerly over the shoes.* MICHAEL MARTIN *takes the shoes away.)*

Anything strange in Killsallagh?

WILLIE. Devil the bit strange only the Doctor's motor-car ran into John Joe McDermott's horse and cart on the Louisburg road this morning and broke the shaft of John Joe's cart and scattered a fine load of mangolds all over the road and John Joe, that's a cousin of my own, let out of him a string of curses would stretch all the way from here to Castlebar. The same Doctor Moran drives that old motor of his as if the devils from hell were inside of him. *(In to* MICHAEL.*)* Going to see Molly Ryan of the Blessed Well he was. She's expecting a baby in April. Are ye all well up here?

MICHAEL. All well, thank God.

WILLIE. Did you ever hear tell of the woman beyond— at "Muck-awn-ither-a-gaw-hallya?—who put out the shoes against the Post-boy? (an' he as holy a man as ever carried the bag)—Well, 'twas how she was expecting a baby—an' the child was born to her that very night—but divil a shoe was ever put on that child's feet—

MARY. 'Twas born without legs?

WILLIE. Cloven hooves!

MICHAEL. Anything strange in Killsallagh?

WILLIE. Strange! Did ye not hear about Dr. Moran?

MARY. No. What?

WILLIE. Didn't he try to murdher me yesterday on the Louisburg road— Oh, as deliberate an attack as was ever made on a government official—came at me from behind—knocked me flat on me ass—scattered me letters to the four winds—a hundred miles an hour he was going—hadn't I to crawl into Louisburg and get twelve stitches in the rear tire of me bicycle?

MICHAEL. The same Dr. Moran drives that old motor car of his as if all the devils of hell were inside of him.

WILLIE. Aye— Rushin' up to the Blessed Well he was to see John Ryan that died sudden in his sleep the night before— How are ye feelin' yourself Michael?

MICHAEL. God between us all an' a sudden death—I'm feeling alright.

WILLIE. Any news of any kind?

MARY. Now, what news could there be up on the mountain? There's never anything strange in Taobh na Cruaiche.

WILLIE. Jamesy Duffy came back from England last night.

(MARY *starts to busy herself stirring the contents of the pot.*)

I stopped to ask him did he ever meet Nora? I have another letter for ye today. *(He takes a letter from bag and looks at the address and postmark in short-sighted manner.)* And it's from the same place as the last one.

MARY. Give it to himself there.

(MICHAEL MARTIN *takes the letter from* WILLIE *and puts it with the other letter on cabinet and crosses to fireplace.*)

Won't you sit down, Willie, and take the weight off your legs.

WILLIE. *(Takes chair Right of table.)* I will, faith, for I'm killed with the climb. *(He sits.)*

MARY. You must have a drop of buttermilk. *(She goes to a pitcher on the cabinet.)*

WILLIE. Sure, let you not bother.

MARY. *(Crossing to above table)* 'Tis nice and fresh. I just churned this morning. It's no bother at all. *(She gives him a cup of buttermilk.)*

WILLIE. Thank you kindly. Is there any word of Nora these days?

MICHAEL. Nora, is it?

MARY. *(Busy about the place.)* She's well enough, thank God. Well enough. She might be coming home for a bit soon.

WILLIE. Well, isn't that grand news! I bet someone down in Killsallagh will be glad to hear that.

MARY. Herself and Anthony Costello was always the best of friends.

MICHAEL. She could have been more to him if she had sense and not be shaking the dust of the mountain off her feet and gallivanting away to England. *(Sits Left of table.)*

WILLIE. Not well, did ye say?

MARY. Oh, well enough, thank God. Well enough.

WILLIE. And sending home plenty of money, no doubt?

(They lean toward WILLIE.)

MICHAEL. Now, who would know that better than yourself that has to carry every letter we get halfway up the mountain?

WILLIE. The letter ye got yesterday wasn't in her handwriting.

MICHAEL. Was it not, now?

WILLIE. Nor the one today either.

    (MARY lifts the pot off the fire, fills a kettle with water and hangs it from the crane.)

It's in London she is, isn't it?

MARY. That's where she used to be.

MICHAEL. But she changed to a better job. 'Twas some place in the country the letter came—

MARY. *(Cutting his short)* But sure they all change. They're never long in the same place.

WILLIE. Was it at service she was?

MARY. Service! Now, what would take Nora to service? She'd turn up her nose at it, she's that independent-like. 'Twas working in a shop she was—a fine, big shop in London.

WILLIE. Oh! Oh! My! My! Are ye not opening the letter?

MARY. Sure, what hurry is there? It's time enough. Patrick can read it for us when he comes in for his tea.

WILLIE. Ah, well— *(Taking a bundle of boxes and odds and ends from his bag)* I tried to get ye some Monastery Herbs, but they're not to be had for love or money. However, these are just as good. "Father Martin's they're called and splendid for the rheumatics. *(Reading from the label)* "For stiff and painful joints and common skin disorders."

MARY. What price are they?

WILLIE. Sixpence to you. A shilling to anyone else.

MARY. I'll take a box, then. *(She goes to a fancy jug on the mantel for the money, takes box with her.)*

WILLIE. I have some safety pins too I picked up in Lahardane and a few pieces of blue and a bag or two of Dolly Varden dyes and, look here, as fine a length of beautiful material as ever you clapped eyes on. *(He displays a length of gaily-coloured material. Moves up Center.)* I bet you haven't seen the like of that since before the war.

MARY. *(Goes up to him.)* Oh, but 'tis very nice.

WILLIE. *(Holding the cloth against MARY KATE)* With a gusset in the bodice and a nice piece of lace to take the plainness off it 'twould make a new woman of you.

(MARY struts down Center with it.)

MICHAEL. Now, what would an old, married woman

like yourself be doing dressed up in the like of that?
(Crosses to fireplace.)

MARY. *(Looking longingly at the cloth, crosses back to*
WILLIE, *then to above table.)* But 'tis very nice all the
same—very fancy— No, Willie. Just give me a piece or
two of the blue.

(WILLIE *gives* MARY KATE *a few pieces of blue and then
takes a small bottle from his bag.)*

WILLIE. Michael Martin, I have here a small sup of
rum out of a barreleen was washed up on Clare Island last
Christmas a year gone. Found by John Thomas Philbin
it was,
(MICHAEL *crosses in.)*
lying on the rocks to the West of the island and of all the
rum and whiskey was washed up during the years of the
war he never saw the beat or equal of it. Half a crown
is all I'll ask you for it.

MARY. Half a crown! Is it rob the people you would?

WILLIE. I'm telling ye now ye won't find the like of that
rum in Stanton's public house or in any public house in
the town of Louisburg or Westport. Why, man, it's that
strong you could float a ship on it.

MICHAEL. Give him two shillings for it.

WILLIE. Two shillings! *(Starts to go.)*

MICHAEL. If the inspector in Westport catches you with
that stuff in your bag you'll find yourself behind prison
bars.

WILLIE. *(Crossing to* MARY) Well, two shillings so.
That'll be two and tenpence altogether. *(To* MICHAEL,
watching as MARY *counts money into his palm.)* The
minute you find the first wheeze coming on you let you
boil it up well with plenty of pepper in it and rub a little
on the outside of your chest as well.
(MARY KATE *takes the bottle.)*
And now I better be on my way. Michael McLoughlin of
the Blessed Well is sick again and I promised to do the

Marthainn Phadraig for them. 'Tis very good for sickness of any kind in man or beast.

MICHAEL. You better be careful Father O'Malley doesn't get on your track for carrying on them heathen practices.

WILLIE. It's only for very special people and for a very special object I do the Marthainn.

MICHAEL. Well, good luck to you anyway.

MARY. And to your patient.

WILLIE. Sure, we can only do our best and trust in God and Saint Patrick.

MICHAEL. And Willie the Post.

WILLIE. *(At the door.)* The wind is rising.

MARY. 'Tis blowing down the chimney and driving the smoke in my eyes.

WILLIE. And the bay is very black-looking. I better be off before the storm comes. Well, whatever it is about Nora, I hope it's nothing serious. Goodbye to ye now. Don't you think you'd ought to read the letter in case there is anything you want me to do?

MICHAEL *and* MARY. Good speed.

(WILLIE *disappears with bicycle,* MICHAEL *shouting after him.)*

WILLIE. *(Off.)* Goodbye now.

(MARY *follows to door.)*

MICHAEL. The same Willie is never happy unless he's managing everyone's affairs. The bride at the wedding. The corpse at the wake. And he's that cute he could herd a litter of mice at a crossroads.

MARY. Open up the letter quick. What does it mean coming so soon after the other?

MICHAEL. *(Gets the letter and sits at table; puts on specs.)* It's from the priest again— She's coming home at once, it seems.

MARY. At once! But when? Doesn't he mention the day?

MICHAEL. It says here she's fixed up for the boat. 'Twas written on a Tuesday and this is Thursday.

MARY. And how long would it take her to travel?

MICHAEL. How would I know. 'Twould take days anyway.

MARY. She'd have the journey on the train and a journey on the sea and then another journey on the train again.

MICHAEL. Everything's in order, it appears— Down here it says "I think we can safely say she will be with you by the end of the week— Yours faithfully, in Jesus Christ, *(Nods.)* Quentin Richardson—"

MARY. *(Absent-mindedly.)* Quentin Richardson—

(ANTHONY COSTELLO *appears at the door. He is a straight, warm-hearted, honest young farmer. He is dressed in the clothes of the fields. His age is about thirty.)*

ANTHONY. God bless all here.

MARY. And you too, Anthony Costello.

MICHAEL. *(Rises.)* Aren't you the stranger? Come in and sit down.

ANTHONY. *(Entering)* What's this I hear about Nora?

MICHAEL. She's coming home all right.

ANTHONY. Isn't that great news? After all these years! Maybe she'll be home in time for the pilgrimage.

(MARY *and* MICHAEL *exchange looks.)*

MARY. She isn't too well, Anthony.

ANTHONY. *(Crosses in to top of table.)* What's wrong with her? Was she hurted in an air raid or what?

MARY. You know as much as we know ourselves.

(Awkward pause.)

MICHAEL. *(Blurts.)* Why don't you tell the lad? Who has a better right to know?

MARY. Let you tell him yourself then.

MICHAEL. What happened was a priest in England to write us she wasn't well. And the letter Willie just brung us says her passage is all fixed up and she's on her way home. He sent word to Father O'Malley too.

MARY. If Father O'Malley had a letter you'd think he'd be up first thing.

MICHAEL. The Parish Priest is a busy man and can't be traipsing up and down the mountain just to please the likes of you and me.

ANTHONY. It couldn't be anything serious or he'd see to it at once so I don't think there's anything to worry about. Maybe he's waiting until she comes home.

(PATRICK *is heard off, whistling at a dog.*)

MARY. *(Crossing to cabinet for egg, then to fireplace)* There's Patrick now. He'll be starving for his tea. *(She boils eggs in a saucepan.)* You'll wait and have a cup of tea with us.

ANTHONY. Ah, sure let ye not bother.

MARY. There's no bother. Sit over.

(ANTHONY *sits Right at table.* MARY *crosses for tea and bread in cabinet.)*

PATRICK. *(Enter* PATRICK *up Center. He is aged about thirty and is a rugged young man. He hangs his cap on the back of the door and sits above table.)* Hello.

ANTHONY. Hello, Patrick.

PATRICK. 'Tisn't often we see you up here now.

ANTHONY. Since Michael went to England I have little time for visiting.

PATRICK. Was that Willie the Post I saw clearing down the road on a bicycle?

MARY. It was. There's another letter from England.

MICHAEL. *(Going to the cabinet for the letter)* He can read it for himself. *(He gives the letter to* PATRICK *and sits again Left of table.)* Why don't you light the lamp? It's getting dark.

(MARY KATE *lights an oil lamp which hangs on the wall near the fireplace.* PATRICK *opens the letter.)*

MARY. How are they all at home, Anthony?

ANTHONY. All well, thank God.

PATRICK. Pulling the devil by the tail, I suppose. Gathering seaweed, burning kelp or, like the rest of us, sowing potatoes on the rocks.

ANTHONY. Sure, as long as we can manage, what have we to complain of? Some people are never done grousing. Never content.

PATRICK. Who'd be content on half a dozen acres of rock with potatoes and salt for your dinner seven days out of seven?

ANTHONY. Better men than you was reared on potatoes. Haven't you a roof to your head, clothes to your back and a fine turf fire to warm your shins by when the day's work is done? Haven't you your health, man, and the strength of a lion in your body? What more do you want?

PATRICK. It's in the pulpit you ought to be—not on the land at all.

MARY. *(Crossing with tea. Pours four cups.)* Men is always arguing. No wonder we have wars. Drink up your tea, let ye.

(MARY KATE *cuts a homemade cake of bread.* PATRICK *and* ANTHONY *have tea.* MICHAEL MARTIN *takes porridge. All bless themselves before eating.* MARY KATE *sits apart at fire and drinks tea.)*

ANTHONY. I was in Westport for the fair. There's great cleaning up and painting of the houses for the pilgrimage.

MARY. Sunday fortnight it's to be, isn't it? You'll be climbing, no doubt?

ANTHONY. I expect so. The Archbishop is to preach at twelve o'clock Mass on the summit.

MARY. I climbed that mountain when I was a girl of fourteen—walking all the way in my bare feet from Letterfrack, away beyond in Connemara. I remember it as if it was yesterday—the old, ruined abbey at Murrisk and a great crowd gathering at the foot of the mountain. Side-cars and brakes and the men from the West with their women sitting behind them. And the standings bright with pictures and prayerbooks. And the hucksters from Westport selling toastcakes and sweets and great, big pots of tea boiling over the smoking turf fires. And then the mist sweeping down from the mountain until the long line of people was gobbled up in it as they climbed on their way to the summit— I was only a young girl then—

PATRICK. I was wondering about Nora. If we should go to Westport to the train or would it be better for her to come on the bus and one of us to meet her at Killsallagh.

MICHAEL. It's hard to know what to do when we don't know the day she's coming.

MARY. It's a lonesome thing, all the same, coming a long journey and no one to meet you. She'll have her box to carry too.

PATRICK. What does Anthony think of it? Did ye show him the letters?

MARY. No, then, we didn't.

PATRICK. (Rises.) And why didn't ye? What, in the name of God, is wrong with ye? Where's that first letter?

MARY. We told him. The letter is there on the dresser.

(PATRICK *takes the first letter from the cabinet and gives the two letters to* ANTHONY *who glances through them.* PATRICK *then goes to the fire and lights a butt of a cigarette with a piece of paper.*)

MICHAEL. Where would she get the money for her passage?

PATRICK. I suppose the priest gave it to her or she saved it out of her earnings. The trouble with the priest is he tells us nothing.

ANTHONY. You'd think she'd write herself.

MICHAEL. *(Rises.)* The storm is rising. I spent half
the day fixing that old roof over our heads. I wish it was
slates and concrete we had instead of yellow wheaten
straw. *(He goes to the door, opens it and looks out into
the storm and up at the thatch. It is now rather dark outside.)*

MARY. *(Crossing to door)* May God grant she won't
sail the seas on a night like this. This time ten years ago,
half Pat Cassidy's land was washed away in a single
night.

ANTHONY. If it keeps on the way it's going the villages
of Murrisk and Lecanvey will soon be no more and the
Atlantic Ocean will be washing against the side of Croagh
Patrick.

(MICHAEL MARTIN *re-enters, closing the door behind
him.)*

PATRICK. If it does the holy pilgrims will have to look
out for a new road to the Kingdom of God.

MICHAEL. Now, none of that talk, you.

PATRICK. *(Crossing to table)* Ah, sure I was only joking. *(To* ANTHONY.*)* Himself there thinks I have no religion at all in my bones. I'm no crawthumper, I know. I
don't spend my time chasing in and out of the chapel, but
I have my own way of looking at things and I'm as good a
believer as the next.

MICHAEL. *(Crossing to fireplace)* I suppose you're all
right and you'll do.

MARY. *(Takes Rosary from wall.)* I hate these wild
nights and the roaring of the sea. May God and His holy
mother look down on all travellers this night. If you're
finished we'll kneel down and say a decade of the Rosary.

(MICHAEL MARTIN *takes Rosary beads from the wall
near the fireplace.* MARY KATE *starts the Rosary in
Irish. The* OTHERS *respond. Through the murmur
the WIND is heard very loud. Suddenly the door
opens. The LIGHT in front of the statue is blown
out.* NORA *is at the door carrying a black box tied*

with rope. She is about twenty-five years of age and is dressed in a coat and hat. She is tired after the journey and the climb and is depressed. The OTHERS *are startled at her entrance.* MARY KATE *runs to meet her.)*

Mother of God! Nora! Agradh mo chroidhe! She's frozen stiff— My poor child! *(She embraces* NORA.*)* We were just talking about you. And there wasn't a soul to meet her! Tch, tch, tch! Why didn't we know you'd be coming? Take that box, will you? (MARY *hands box to* MICHAEL.)

NORA. How are you, Father?

MICHAEL. I'm grand, thanks.

PATRICK. Hello, Nora.

NORA. Hello, Patseen— Anthony! Fancy you being here!

(ANTHONY *goes to* NORA; *impulsively kisses her.)*

ANTHONY. *(Embarrassed.)* You're welcome home, Nora. We were—they were waiting for you—a long time waiting.

(Pause. The first tension over, they ALL *blabber together.)*

MICHAEL. If only we knew she was coming we might have made arrangements, but if people doesn't think it worth their while to make it clear—

MARY. We were just saying a prayer you'd be safe on the sea. Wasn't it queer the door opening in the middle of our prayers? You'd imagine it was the hand of—

(Simultaneously.)

PATRICK. I'd have gone myself to the bus to meet you and saved you all that journey up the hill with your box. I know you'd have liked someone to meet you. But how were we to know—

MARY. *(Taking off* NORA'S *coat)* Will ye look at the finery of her! *(Admiring* NORA'S *coat)* There's great weight in that cloth. Ah, sure the best is not too good for you, alannah. *(Crosses Left with* NORA.) Come over to the fire and sit down. You must be dead tired carrying your box up the mountain.

NORA. *(Helped to the fire by* MARY KATE, *where she sits.)* I am tired.

MARY. If only you had left it below, Patrick could have gone down for it in the morning. Weren't you the very foolish girl now! Where's that tongs? *(She fusses with the fire.)*

NORA. I didn't want any fuss or trouble. I've been trouble enough already.

MARY. Ah, you've lost the bloom of health in your cheeks. *(To* MICHAEL MARTIN.) Will you go out and get a brestle of turf. She's stiff with the cold.

(Exit MICHAEL MARTIN *Center.)*

(MARY KATE *rubs* NORA'S *hands.)* What happened you at all? (MARY *crosses to cabinet for egg; then to fireplace.)*

ANTHONY. *(Crosses in to above table.)* She was just saying before you came in about the awful night it was to travel. We didn't know whether it was better to go to Westport to meet the bus. It was how we were all confused.

(MARY KATE *is bustling about. She puts the kettle on the fire and boils an egg in a saucepan.)*

PATRICK. *(Apologetic concern.)* No one could make out when you were coming. 'Twas the way the letter was writ.

NORA. I managed well enough. And I'm home again.— It's queer how small the kitchen seems. And the hearth that seemed so big? *(Rises to down Left.)* Mother, I wish you'd stay quiet and not be rushing around.

MARY. *(Moving to table)* Now, I'll have a cup of tea ready for you in a minute and a nice drop of cream and a fresh, boiled egg. Sure you must be famished.

NORA. I'll be all right now. I know I'll be all right because I'm at home. *(She looks hungrily around the kitchen. Going to fireplace)* Ireland, he said, is a holy place—the backbone of Christianity.

MARY. —Who said that, Nora?

(NORA *does not reply. Re-enter* MICHAEL MARTIN *with an armful of turf. He stands watching* NORA, *then goes to fireplace.)*

NORA. I don't know what I'd have done only for Father Richardson. I was alone for so long—shut up in myself—I couldn't make a friend of anyone. *(She stops when she sees her father.)* Yes, he was very kind to me. He seemed to know what was the matter. *(Sits Left of table.)*

MICHAEL. *(Crossing to top of fireplace)* Your mother had herself worried to death for the past year about you. It was a queer way for a daughter of hers to behave. If it was only the writing on the envelope itself. You might be dead as far as we knew, getting the *Mayo News* every week and reading about bombs and destruction everywhere. 'Twas no way for a daughter to behave.

MARY. Now, a cup of tea is nearer than the door and you mustn't upset her before she's had something to put the life in her body. Anthony, will you sit down and not be standing up. *(Pulls chair for* ANTHONY.)

(ANTHONY *sits Right of table.)*

Have you no word of welcome at all for Nora? (MARY *crosses to cabinet.)*

ANTHONY. They were all wondering, below, not hearing anything about you for so long. You wrote an awful lot at first and then you stopped altogether.

NORA. They're not looking after you, Anthony. You got thinner. Or maybe you're just grown up now—we seemed to be so young then.

ANTHONY. I'm working harder, Nora. We've more tillage to do now and since Michael went to America I haven't a minute to spare. You got thinner yourself, Nora. England mustn't have agreed with you.

NORA. Yes, it isn't every one it agrees with. It's a great change, of course, but there's a lot you miss—the rain, the mountains, the friendly word—

ANTHONY. And yet everyone coming back talks of the wild life and excitement of the cities.

NORA. *(Turns away.)* Do you remember the races at Murrisk and the horses chasing through the rising tide? We were there the day before I left.

ANTHONY. *(Pause.)* We have the races still, Nora.

NORA. Yes, there's a lot you miss.

MARY. *(Crossing to above NORA)* Now have your tea.

(There are tea, bread and butter and a boiled egg on table.)

NORA. I'm not hungry. I had a cup of tea in Westport waiting for the bus.

MARY. The tea you get in a tearoom is never the same as you get at home. So drink up now. 'Twill put new life in you. Sit over, Anthony. Keep her company and have a cup of tea too. Ah, it must be a long tiresome journey from England. When did you start on your way?

NORA. I left yesterday morning.

MARY. And where did you spend the night?

NORA. In Dublin—in a hotel. But I didn't mind. A kind of a peace came over me and I coming off the boat. This is Ireland now, I said to myself. My father and mother and Patrick—and Anthony—they're all here.

(They ALL move in.)

I'm going to get well. I'll have all the protection I need. *(Rises.)* I'll rise out of the valley of the shadow of death—

PATRICK. What do you mean—the valley of the shadow of death? What kind of talk is that?

(NORA does not reply.)

ANTHONY. Has none of ye noticed the stylish way she speaks? Bedad, she wasn't long picking up the grand accent.

MARY. 'Tis nice, all the same, her way of speaking—like Mrs. O'Rourke, the dentist's wife in Louisburg.

ANTHONY. *(Jokingly)* But Mrs. O'Rourke is an Englishwoman. I think this lassie here is only putting it on. Sure, it's only the other day she left Taobh na Cruaiche.

PATRICK. 'Tis two years surely.

MARY. 'Tis near two years, son.

NORA. 'Tis two years and one month exactly. It was the fifteenth of August I left, the Feast of the Assumption of the Blessed—

ANTHONY. Yes, the feast of the Assumption of the Blessed Virgin.

MARY. The fair of Murrisk was on—the day after the races. We could see the standings from here and the crowd gathering as we came out to give her God-speed. Patrick went with her to the bus while himself and myself stayed behind to save hay. Ah, it was a fine, dry day.

ANTHONY. What's wrong, Nora?

NORA. Nothing— I suppose you think it queer my coming home like this. I heard ye at the Rosary before I opened the door.

ANTHONY. Do ye hear that? "Door" she says, just like the dentist's wife. Before long, half the people in Killsallagh will be talking like the English. Before the war it used to be the Yankee accent but now it's the English. God, won't we be the grand people!

NORA. *(Attempting to shake off her depression)* Go on out of that with you, Anthony Costello. You're as bad a joker as ever you were. But it'll take more than a grand accent to make a lady out of me. *(Sits in chair Right of table.)*

ANTHONY. Ha, ha!! She wasn't long getting back her old form. She's as quick with the tongue as ever.

NORA. Oh, I don't know. I've been through a lot. I'm tired.

MICHAEL. *(Crossing to NORA)* You didn't tell us yet why you stopped writing. Your sisters in America never left it that long. I can't understand what all the mystery is about.

MARY. Don't mind himself, Nora. Finish your tea. (*Crosses down to* MICHAEL.)

MICHAEL. But I have a right to know. To send a pound regular every week and then to stop all of a sudden. It's not that I mind the money but it's as plain as a pikestaff there was some upset or other and I'm demanding now to know what that upset was.

NORA. There was so much to see and do. I was never in England before. And you get tired writing. You know I always hated anything to do with books or pens. And then there was the war and bombs dropping in London and everything terrible uncertain.

MICHAEL. It wasn't from London the priest's letter came.

NORA. I got an offer of a better job in Lancashire six months ago and I left London. And when I got there I wasn't feeling well.

MICHAEL. What was the matter with you?

NORA. The doctor said it was my nerves.

MARY. Your nerves, alannah?

MICHAEL. I hope it was nothing else.

NORA. It was nothing else.

MICHAEL. What are you keeping back then? We're your own flesh and blood. What are you hiding from us?

MARY. If it was anything wrong you done we'll understand you and forgive you.

NORA. There's nothing I can tell you. There's nothing for you to forgive.

MICHAEL. (*Crossing to above table*) What brung you to Lancashire at all? Earning good money in London I can see no reason for leaving it.

NORA. London was too great a strain on me. I couldn't stand the noise. I couldn't stand the talk of fire and floods and people trapped in shelters.

MICHAEL. (*Questioning closely*) What kind of a job did you go to?

NORA. Oh, I went to service.

(Exchange of family looks.)

MICHAEL. Service?

NORA. I didn't mind what I worked at as long as I was paid for it. There's little foolish pride left in me now, I'm telling you. It was there I got sick—in Wallsend. And then I was moved—

MICHAEL. *(Sharply.)* Where were you moved to?

(NORA *makes no reply.)*

ANTHONY. A person that's travelled all the way from England is tired and shouldn't be excited. *(Crosses to side of* NORA.)

MICHAEL. *(Crossing to fireplace)* I'm not going to rest until I hear the ins and outs of all this. She brung nothing but talk and trouble on the house for the past six months. Her mother there never done worrying and none of us able to go to Mass in Lecanvey or to the market in Louisburg without having to tell a string of lies and falsehoods to the neighbours about how she was getting on and all the money she was sending home.

NORA. *(High.)* You're as hard on me as ever you were. Isn't it enough to tell you I was sick and had to have a doctor?

MICHAEL. But where does the priest come into it? I hope to Almighty God— *(Sarcastically.)* Ah— *(Hands up.)*

(NORA *cries quietly.)*

MARY. Look now what you've done!

ANTHONY. *(Rises; crosses to her.)* Don't cry, Nora. You're a queer, wild man, Michael Martin Geraty. *(To* NORA, *hands on her arms.)* Hail, rain or snow, nothing makes any difference to me. To me you're the same Nora that left Taobh na Cruaiche two years ago. I'll be on my way now but I'll be up to see you soon again.

NORA. Goodbye, Anthony.

PATRICK. I'll see you on to the road. *(Crosses up Center and out.)*

ANTHONY. The old bike will have me down in no time. God protect you, Nora.

(But MICHAEL MARTIN *and* MARY KATE *are too distraught to reply. After a look at* NORA, ANTHONY *exits with* PATRICK. *As they go out the STORM is heard.* MARY KATE *clears the table.)*

MARY. Carry her box into the back room, will you, and take that rope off it. I think I'd better sleep in there with her tonight.

(Exit MICHAEL MARTIN *with the box up Left.* NORA *rises.* MARY KATE *moves chair to fireplace.* NORA *sits at fire.)*

Take off your shoes, asthore, and warm your feet at the fire. Here, let me do it for you. *(She kneels, removes* NORA's *sshoes and rubs her feet. Sits Right of* NORA.) Don't mind, agradh. He has a rough tongue but he's fond of you. Poor men has little time for softness.

NORA. He never liked me— The homeliness of the turf fire! The warm light of it on the floor! I never want to see England again.

MARY. *(Holding aloft one of* NORA's *shoes. Joking)* Isn't it a wonder now you'd waste hard-earned money on them fancy, high-heeled shoes and money so scarce? Little use they'll be to you in the rocky fields of Taobh no Cruaiche.

NORA. Heavy boots and nailed shoes might be alright in Taobh na Cruaiche but they're little use to you in England. Besides, you want to smarten yourself up a bit nowadays if you want to get anywhere. That much I learned since I left. I'm a different girl, you know.

MARY. And sure, maybe, they'll be of use to you if you go back again. Or do you mean to go back at all?

NORA. I don't know. I don't know what to think. There's not much life for me in Taobh na Cruaiche—rocks and stone walls, poverty and drudgery. I ask you, what other life is there?

MARY. *(Looking around her home)* Little, I suppose, except maybe marriage and settling down with the right man. After all, there's great contentment in marriage.

NORA. Poor Anthony! The fool I used to make of him! But, somehow or other, this evening, immediately I saw him my heart warmed to him. He's simple and nice—and good-looking. I never noticed it before. I'm wondering if he meant what he said— I mean, about me being the same to him as ever I was. I wonder what it would be like—married to Anthony Costello.

MARY. I don't know. Men have the say in them matters. But there's some things a man can hardly close his eyes to—some things that no one would expect him to close his eyes to. Tell me, Nora, for God's sake, what was the matter with you?

NORA. *(Exasperated.)* Why must you bother me like this? *(High.)* First him, now you! I'm sorry I ever came home. *(Then regretting her outburst)* There now, I've made you cry. I'm sorry, Mother. I've been through hell. I'm awful tired and it's more than I can stand.

MARY. *(Rising)* All right, so. I won't ask you any more questions. May God and His holy mother watch over us this night!—The lamp is gone out with the wind.

(She lights the lamp in front of the statue. NORA, with her back to the statue, at once reacts to the lighting of the lamp. A dizzy feeling is succeeded by a choking one.)

NORA. *(Sharply. In a hoarse voice.)* Put out that light.
MARY. What did you say?
NORA. Put out the lamp.
MARY. *(At table.)* The lamp?
NORA. *(Jumping up)* The lamp before the statue.
MARY. What's the matter with you?
   (NORA faces her mother. Her back is to the audience. She groans deeply.)
(MARY KATE is startled by the look in her face. Weakly.) Michael Martin! *(Then loudly.)* Michael Martin!

MICHAEL. *(Enters.)* Yes!! *(He sees* NORA *and is startled.)* What's wrong with you?

NORA. Oui per Immaculatum Virginis Conceptionem dignum Filio tuo habitaculum praeparasti. *(She is facing the statue and gives a shrill laugh.)* Put out that lamp. Why do you torment me? Put it out! Put it out!! Put it out!!!

MARY. *(Opening the door and shouting out into the night, in terror)* Patrick! Patrick!!

NORA. *(At Center.)* Put-it-out—put—put-it-out.

MICHAEL. Put out the lamp, for God's sake.

(MARY KATE *puts out the lamp.* PATRICK *enters. Comes to table.)*

PATRICK. What's happened? *(Then seeing* NORA*)* What's wrong with her?

MARY. I don't know, son. I can't make it out. I just lit the lamp before the statue and a sudden change came over me.

PATRICK. *(Crosses to her. Trying to take* NORA *out of the trance)* Nora —Nora— Do you hear me? It's me— Patrick—your brother— Look at me— *(He lifts head. He draws away from her.)* Nora! Nora!

NORA. *(Turns. She glances at the* OTHERS *and, with a little laugh, speaks.)* I've upset you now. I've frightened you. Please forgive me. I lost control of myself. You can call it a joke if you like.

MICHAEL. If it was a a joke it was a foolish one. Holy things should be treated with respect, not with shouting and screaming like a drunker tinker at a fair.

MARY. But the lamp! *(Moves down to table Left.)* To behave so queer about the lamp in front of the statue of Our Lady! Daughter, what was it? What came over you?

NORA. *(Pause. With cunning, quietly and convincingly.)* I suppose I'm different *(Goes up Right.)* to what you are. Lately I've been thinking that lamps and statues and prayers don't count for much in the long run. Even Father Richardson was saying that religion goes much deeper than that. We waste too much time on the trimmings, he said, and not enough on the things that matter. We can't see the wood for the trees, were the very words he used.

MARY. But we've always lit the lamp in front of the statue or the picture of the Sacred Heart. They've statues and pictures in the chapel. I don't understand it at all.

NORA. And maybe people can be too much taken up with religion—choked and strangled by it—with too much praying and worship of angels and saints. It doesn't get you far nowadays. Patrick should know what I mean. He spent some time in England too.

(PATRICK *goes to the window and looks out.*)
That's why we're all so poor in this country. *(Sits at table up Right.)* We're taught to believe that it's as difficult for a rich man to get into heaven as it is for a camel to pass through the eye of a needle. We're listening to that sort of talk from the day we're born till the day we die—hoping against hope that it's good to be poor and that riches and prosperity will come our way in the afterlife they tell us about. Afterlife? Who can tell for sure if there is an afterlife?

MICHAEL. *(Crossing to* NORA) There's a lot of that talk we don't understand. It's not what we're used to. Where did you get all that learning? Who have you been listening to?

NORA. I've discovered that I have a mind of my own. I've learned to think for myself| I never believe anything now unless my reason tells me it's true. What use is our reason otherwise? Patrick there agrees with everything I say. Don't you, Patrick?

PATRICK. This is no place for that kind of talk.

NORA. And himself too has a feeling that what I say is true. What has he got for a lifetime of honesty and religion? A few acres of rock on the side of a mountain and his family scattered to the four corners of the earth.

MICHAEL. There's very little comfort in life, it's true.

MARY. Haven't you your wife and a fine, strong son? Aren't you the master of the fields around your home?

Haven't you the comfort and hope of your religion?
Haven't you the peace of God in your heart?

MICHAEL. Maybe I have. Maybe I haven't.

NORA. *(Rises; crosses to upstage above table.)* Poverty
follows on the trail of religion. I know.

MARY. *(Crossing to her)* For God's sake stop it. Put an
end to that evil talk at once or you'll drive me mad. If
you weren't my daughter I'd turn you out of the house at
once. *(Crosses to Center.)*

PATRICK. *(Crosses to above table Left.)* Let her talk.
Let her talk if she wants to. There was always too much
browbeating in this house.

NORA. Browbeating—that's the trouble. You mustn't
think for yourselves. Believe everything they tell you—
heaven, hell and the mysteries of religion! Faith, faith,
faith! But they don't tell you that faith is blind—that
faith breeds slaves and cowards.

MARY. Stop it. Stop that blasphemy or you'll bring the
wrath of God on our heads. You'll be turning your father
and brother against their religion too.

MICHAEL. *(Rises, with look to MARY.)* Let the girl be.
Hasn't she a right to speak out what's in her mind? I'm
wondering if there isn't something in what she says.

MARY. Now, see what she's doing to you! She's turning
you against your God and your religion. Put her out before I strike her. *(She runs at her.)*

(PATRICK *stops her.)*

(On her knees before her husband.) Put her out. Put her
out.

NORA. I'll not go.

MARY. *(Moving Left to bedroom)* You'll not stay a
minute longer under this roof. I'll get your box this instant.
(She exits to the room.)

NORA. *(Turns up.)* I'll never leave this house. *(In a
trance.)* I'll take possession of it and of every soul belonging to it.

(Re-enter MARY KATE with NORA's box.)

The priest knows all about me. He's had a letter and he'll
climb the mountain to talk to me. But I'll not see him. I'll

not see him. *(She walks slowly across the stage, turns suddenly opposite the statue, goes quickly to it, takes it in her hands and holds it aloft. Mockingly.)* Benedicta es tu, Virgo Maria, a Domino Deo excelo prae omnibus mulieribus suptr terram! *(She spits on the statue and dashes it to the ground. In a frenzy.)* There is no God! There is no God!

MARY. *(Speaking through* NORA'S *speech)* She's out of her mind. She's raving. She's gone mad.

(NORA *collapses on the floor.)*

(MARY KATE *runs to her and kneels.)* Go for the doctor and Father O'Malley at once. Hurry! Hurry!

(PATRICK *runs out.)*

CURTAIN

(End of Act One.)

ACT TWO

Scene as in Act One. It is an hour or two later. NORA *is asleep on the bed.* MARY KATE *is removing clothes from* NORA'S *valise and is airing them at the fire.* MICHAEL MARTIN *sits brooding at the fireplace.*

MICHAEL. If it was rich people we were they'd be here long ago.

MARY. *(Whispers as she hangs garments.)* That's no way to talk of the priest. The danger is over anyway, whatever it was, and she's sleeping like a lamb.

MICHAEL. I can't understand her throwing a fit and then, of a sudden, all signs of it to leave her.

MARY. *(At fireplace.)* It was a mad fit. She was raving all the time and I didn't know it. I should have more understanding in me. Her clothes are wet through from the journey. *(She puts some of* NORA'S *clothes on a line which hangs under the mantelpiece.)* We can put her to bed proper when they've seen her.

MICHAEL. Mad he'll be now bringing him up that long way and nothing the matter with her. *(Crosses up.)*

MARY. *(Crossing up to bed)* Father O'Malley'll not mind when we tell him all. He's a man with great understanding in him. She's sleeping terrible sound. The innocent face of her in the bed! You'd never think she could utter them dreadful things.

MICHAEL. *(Left of bed.)* What do you suppose what's all them marks on her arm.

MARY. I don't know. They're all over her body. They're kinda bruises, I think.

MICHAEL. *(Goes to door; opens; looks out.)* The night is long when there's sickness in the house. You better sweep up that rubbish and throw it out before the priest comes. *(Crosses back to fireplace.)*

34

(MARY KATE *stands and looks for a moment at the remains of the statue. She then takes a brush and sweeps it into a heap. She then throws it in handfuls into the fire.*)

MARY. Blessed things should be burned—not thrown out to the four winds of heaven to be trampled by the beasts in the field. That statue must be in the house a long time.

MICHAEL. It was there as long as I can remember. And I a child, Sarah Ann would put flowers in front of it of a May Eve—mayflowers she'd pluck at the stream beyond and put in a jug in front of the statue and throw a heap more on the threshold outside.

MARY. *(Kneeling at valise with clothes)* The people that's gone were holy. *(Makes sign of the cross.)*

MICHAEL. Ah, I don't know. The people that's gone went on with a lot of old nonsense and superstitions.

MARY. *(Giving him a look)* You get used to a thing in the house and you miss it when it's gone. What evil came over her? *(Rises.)* What made her dash it to the ground in pieces? Does she want to bring bad luck down on ourselves and all belonging to us?

(NORA *is awakened by the sound of her voice and sits up in bed.*)

MICHAEL. *(Right of bed.)* You've wakened her now, so you have.

(MICHAEL MARTIN *and* MARY KATE *both look at* NORA *with apprehension.* NORA *acts normally, like a person wakened from a sound sleep. She sees her* PARENTS.)

NORA. What are you standing there for—looking at me?

MARY. We were wondering—we were hoping you were all right.

NORA. All right?—I must have fallen asleep.

MARY. Yes. You were tired.

NORA. I fainted?

MARY. It must be a long, fatiguing journey from England.

NORA. *(Rises in bed.)* But nothing out of the ordinary —nothing strange happened?

MICHAEL. We thought you were sickening for something and we sent Patrick down for Doctor Moran.

NORA. But I'm all right now. I only fainted— Anyone can collapse like that. You shouldn't have sent for the doctor. You're making too much fuss over nothing. I don't want to see any doctor. I don't want to see anyone. *(Sitting up.)*

MICHAEL. Coming that long way and not seeing you for two years how were we to know you weren't in danger? He's coming anyway and you'll have to see him. You better make up your mind to that.

NORA. Oh, I suppose there's no way out of it.

(PARENTS *move in and grab her as she falls.)*
My head— it feels heavy— The turf smoke, I suppose— There's a sort of cloud in my brain— So, I fainted?

MARY. Yes. Don't you remember?

NORA. *(Crossing to Right slowly)* Kinda. But I don't want to talk about it— You've still got the old, cracked dishes on the dresser. We'll have to go to Westport next fair day and get some nice cups and saucers at John Gibbons'. I saved a little money when I was in England. We'll all go to the fair and have a day's outing. And I want to go to the dances again at Bunowen and Louisburg. They used to be great fun in the old days. *(Going to her valise and taking out a frock)* I'll knock them all flat with a few dresses I brought home with me. What do you think of that one? *(She holds out the dress in front of her.)* A quid in a secondhand shop in Berwick Market—in London that is.

MARY. 'Tis very nice but skimpy, I'd say.

NORA. *(Goes again to valise.)* It's nothing to this. *(She shows another. Crossing to Center. To MARY.)* I got it

from a girl who was going to India. She was so sorry for
me that time I fell sick—

MARY. Yes, alannah? *(Crosses Right to MICHAEL.)*

*(During these speeches NORA is moving restlessly about
in an effort to clear her brain and collect her
thoughts.)*

NORA. *(Crossing to door Center)* It's time too we had
a decent slated roof over our heads. *(Opens door.)* That
old thatch is awful—tying it down with rocks and ropes
to stop the wind from the mountain sweeping it into the
middle of Clew Bay.

MICHAEL. *(Crossing down Left a bit)* A slated roof costs
money and you can't get money on the side of the road.

NORA. They might send us help—if we wrote to them
in America. *(Pause.)* By the way, when did this happen?
(Pause.) I mean, when did Patrick go for the doctor?

MARY. About an hour ago.

NORA. I see— Yes, the same old kitchen. It's homely,
though. And solid and friendly—like the rocks around us.
And the settle that grandfather used to say came off a
Spanish ship that was wrecked off Clare Island!—What
happened the statue?

(MICHAEL MARTIN is looking into the fire.)

MARY. *(Sits up Right.)* It broke. It fell to the ground
off the shelf and was broke.

NORA. And himself was that proud of it. The shelf looks
so bare now. Never mind. We'll get another at the next
mission in Westport.

(MICHAEL MARTIN and MARY KATE are puzzled.)
(Crossing to above table Left) The heaviness is leaving
my head. How do I look, in the name of goodness? *(She
is looking in a small mirror which is hanging on the wall.)*
Tch! I look an awful wreck. I'm like something that slept
all night in a cock of hay, or a tinker's wife under a cart,
or poor old Mary Ann Scrape all the way from Castlebar.

(She furiously combs her hair.) Doctor or no doctor, I'll look a wreck in front of no man. *(She takes a powder box from a pocket in her skirt.)* I don't care whether you're shocked or not, I'm putting on a load of this stuff.

MARY. *(Rises. Crossing to Center)* No respectable girl paints and plasters her face. You'll be like a circus woman. What would the neighbours say?

NORA. *(Crossing in to her)* The neighbours can say what they like. I'll plaster as much as I want to.

MICHAEL. Isn't it time you asked her about them marks?

(MICHAEL MARTIN *and* MARY KATE *exchange looks.)*

NORA. What marks?

MARY. On your arms and your body, daughter. You're bruised all over. I loosened your clothes when you fainted.

NORA. *(Leans into her.)* There are things happened in England I don't want to remember. I'm at home now. I came home to get my health. So, for heaven's sake, give me a chance and don't keep hammering questions at me at every hand's turn.

MARY. But the way you spoke of God and the Faith and religion!

NORA. What did I say about Faith and religion?

MARY. The way it was no use any more—when you took the queer turn—before you fainted—just when I lit the lamp before the statue. Don't you remember?

NORA. What exactly did I say?

MARY. *(Looks at* MICHAEL MARTIN.) You were trying to turn us all against everything holy—that we were wasting our time. You upset himself and Patrick there something terrible. You carried on like a thing half mad. You took the statue and smashed it to the ground. That's what happened the statue, daughter.

NORA. *(In misery, kneels at fireplace. Gazes up at painting.)* Oh, God, God, God! Keep this evil away from our house—away from my own people—away from my mother and father and Patrick. *(She faces them, distraught. Turn-*

ing to MARY KATE, *goes above table.)* I was mad. It has
to do with my illness. I lose control over myself. If it
happens again you must pay no attention to anything I
say or do. *(Suddenly on the alert.)*

> *(The SOUND of a car is heard through the storm.*
> MICHAEL MARTIN *exits by the Center door, closing
> it after him.)*

(NORA *rises.)* The doctor, I suppose?

MARY. *(Goes to door.)* I don't know—it might be the
doctor—or it might be—you see, we told Patrick—

NORA. Who might it be if it's not the doctor? Father
O'Malley, I suppose. You sent for the priest? *(Crossing
to Left.)*

MARY. You were sick. I think you should lie down on
the cailleach. The doctor is a hot-tempered man and might
be angry with us sending down for him that long way and
you walking about as if there was nothing the matter with
you.

NORA. I'll sit by the fire. Why should I lie down if I'm
not sick? And I'm not sick. There's nothing he can do for
me. *(She sits by the fire.)*

(Enter DOCTOR MORAN. *He is a bluff, country doctor,
fond of his roast of beef and a good ball of malt. He
dresses in tweeds. Age about fifty-five.)*

DOCTOR. *(To* PATRICK *who is outside.)* Switch off those
lights, young fellow.

PATRICK. *(Off.)* I will, Doctor.

DOCTOR. *(To* MICHAEL MARTIN, *who has entered with
him.)* Isn't it time you people levelled off that old rocky
yard of yours? I nearly broke my neck in the dark.

MICHAEL. *(At door.)* 'Tis hard to level the bare moun-
tainside.

MARY. Take the doctor's coat, will you. Where's your
manners?

DOCTOR. *(Throwing his hat on a chair up Right. Turns
to* MARY KATE.) You needn't bother. Well, where is she?
(Puts bag on table Left.)

MARY. *(Backing up to fire.)* She's here by the fire, Doctor. She's just after waking and getting up off the cailleach.

DOCTOR. Just after waking!

MARY. When she fainted we put her lying down and she went off to sleep at once.

DOCTOR. *(Crosses to above table Left.)* And do you mean to say you dragged me half way up the side of Croagh Patrick to attend a silly woman that's fainted?

NORA. I told them they shouldn't have bothered sending for you.

PATRICK. *(Entering to between* DOCTOR *and* MICHAEL MARTIN*)* You're all right, Nora?

DOCTOR. Will you look at her, for God's sake! *(Takes bag from table. Turns to leave.)* What sort of fools are living up here at the back of beyond? There's a saying down below that the people of Taobh na Cruaiche are half goats. I never believed it before. But I do now. Do ye know this is a time of emergency and petrol and tyres are scarcer than grass on the mountain? *(Starts rummaging in his bag.)*

MICHAEL. *(Surly.)* The girl was sick. Didn't you hear what herself said? She was raving.

NORA. It's no use going into all that with the doctor.

MICHAEL. *(Surly.)* We wouldn't send for you unless we thought she was bad. Mountainy people is poor and has to be careful of their pence and halfpence. She took a queer turn.

MARY. As himself says, she was raving.

PATRICK. It's a doctor's duty to attend to them that's sick—rich or poor.

DOCTOR. *(Crossing to on a line with* PATRICK.*)* Do I hear aright and has the U.S.S.R. come to Taobh na Cruaiche? None of your Bolshevik ideas with me, young man, or I'll give you my bag straight across the face.

MARY. We're sorry, Doctor, and we beg your pardon. But we were afeard.

DOCTOR. *(Softening)* Very well so, woman. Sure you

know I don't mean a word of what I say. I might as well
have a look at her as I'm here.

MARY. She only come home from England this evening.

DOCTOR. *(With meaning.)* Oh, from England, did she?
Why didn't you say so at first?

(NORA *looks at him.*)

Take her into the bedroom till I have a look at her.

MARY. 'Tis cold in there, Doctor. Maybe you better
examine her here where there's heat from the fire. *(Places
chair for him.)*

DOCTOR. You fellows get out then.

MICHAEL. Men that's used to dealing with the beasts in
the field doesn't mind watching their own. *(Crosses in.)*

DOCTOR. Get out.

(Exit MICHAEL MARTIN *and* PATRICK *by the Center
door.)*

(DOCTOR *takes a stethosocope from his bag. Pulls up chair
and sits facing* NORA.) What part of England were you
in?

NORA. *(Gloomily)* In London—for a while. Then I went
North—to Lancashire.

DOCTOR. Were you under doctor's care there?

NORA. I was.

DOCTOR. Did you bring a medical report with you?

NORA. No. I didn't.

DOCTOR. Did you get into any trouble?

MARY. What kind of trouble?

NORA. It's all right, Mother. I know what he means. No,
Doctor. There's nothing like that the matter with me. If
there was I'd tell you. It's something to do with my nerves
—it's hard to explain—he was an English doctor—was
attending me—a Doctor Wilkinson—a young man. What
he said was he couldn't understand it proper but •he
thought my nerves must be upset.

DOCTOR. I see. Come over here and sit on the chair.

(NORA *sits on chair, Center.* MARY KATE *crosses
above table to Left of her.)*

Do you often faint like this?

NORA. No. Not often.

DOCTOR. Open up that blouse of yours. There, lean back now. *(He stands in front of her and examines her with the stethoscope.)* Breathe— Go on breathing— Sound enough, faith. *(He pulls down her eyelids and examines them.)* —Plenty of spuds and cabbage, milk, butter and eggs. That's what she wants. *(To* MARY KATE.*)* The girl's a bit run-down. That's all. And who wouldn't be, coming from that land of starvation across the water? Yes, send the boy to me in the morning and I'll give him a bottle for her. *(He moves Right of her, then takes her pulse and, while doing so, notices the bruises on her arm.)* How did that happen?

(NORA *does not answer.)*

(Pointing) Where did those marks come from?

MARY. She has them on her shoulders and breast and all over her body.

DOCTOR. *(Examining her arm and bared shoulder)* Were you in an air raid?

(NORA *does not answer.)*

(Holding her arm) I say, how did you get those?

NORA. I was in several air raids in London. *(Rising. Crossing Right.)*

DOCTOR. And didn't your doctor say anything about them? Some of them seem to me to be quite fresh. Did he see them at all?

NORA. He didn't seem to know. I tried to tell him but he said he couldn't understand.

DOCTOR. *(Crossing to* NORA*)* What couldn't he understand?

NORA. *(Excitedly.)* All about *her* and the way she used to trouble me. And why she troubled no one else but me.

DOCTOR. What are you talking about?

NORA. *(Looking at her mother. Crosses back to chair; sits.)* I'm talking—he's exciting me— I don't know what I'm saying. *(She bursts into tears and cries bitterly.)*

(They allow her to cry for a while.)

MARY. You mustn't cry like that, Nora.

DOCTOR. You're keeping something from me, whatever it is. How do you expect me to prescribe for you if you're not candid with me?

MARY. Why don't you tell him, Nora?

NORA. *(Trance-like. Rises; crosses down Right.)* What good would it do if I opened up my heart and soul to you? That wouldn't bring me peace—the peace I'm looking for. Besides, he's nearly here now. He's coming in his car up the road. Do you hear it? Do you hear it?

(The OTHERS *listen. From now until* PATRICK'S *entrance* NORA *is in a trance.)*

MARY. I hear nothing, Doctor. Do you?

NORA. He's rounding the turn by the big rock. I mustn't see him because whenever his kind approaches me it begins to happen. So, I mustn't see him. He's not to come near me.

MARY. But you must see him. We sent for him. We thought you were dying.

NORA. He's almost here now. He knows all about me. He'll tell you all because he's had a letter. But I'll give him no information because I don't like him. He's my enemy. He's against my kind.

MARY. How do you mean—your kind—daughter?

PATRICK. *(Enters. At door.)* That's like the priest's car now. It's coming up the boreen.

NORA. *(In an outburst of terror.)* I told ye. Didn't I? I won't have him near me. You're not going to let him cross the threshold. I don't want him to see me. I'll have nothing to do with him. (NORA *runs into the kitchen.)*

DOCTOR. Go after her and keep an eye on her. And don't be too pressing about her coming out when Father O'Malley is here. Give way to her for a bit. She's overwrought.

(Exit MARY KATE *after* NORA. *The* DOCTOR *puts away his stethoscope thoughtfully and looks after* MARY KATE *and* NORA. FATHER O'MALLEY *appears at the Center door.* MICHAEL MARTIN *is behind him. The* PRIEST

is a fine-looking man, grey-haired. Age about sixty.
He is a strong, spiritual type.)

PRIEST. *(Stopping at the door, as he feels the presence*
of something strange, evil and terrifying. He looks around
the kitchen before he speaks. He enters and takes off his
hat and coat.)
　　(MICHAEL MARTIN *takes them from him.)*
(To MICHAEL MARTIN.) Thank you. *(To the* DOCTOR.)
Where is she? *(To table Left.)*
　　DOCTOR. She's in there with her mother.
　　(As the PRIEST *moves towards the room door, then*
to fireplace.)
(To PATRICK.) Go and throw something over the radiator
of the priest's car. It's a cold night up here in the clouds.
　　(PATRICK *exits.)*
(Crossing to door. Shouting) And throw an old sack over
mine too. And you needn't be in too much of a hurry
coming back. *(To* MICHAEL MARTIN.) And you go in
there to your wife. We'll call you when we want you.

(Exit MICHAEL MARTIN *to the bedroom.)*

　　PRIEST. *(Crossing in)* Have you examined her?
　　DOCTOR. Yes. There's nothing very much the matter—
a bit overtired and highly-strung, perhaps—but, for some
reason or other, she threw a tantrum when she heard you
were coming.
　　PRIEST. *(Thoughtfully.)* I understand.
　　DOCTOR. *(Crossing to fireplace)* What do you mean?
　　PRIEST. *(But the* PRIEST *is looking thoughtfully into*
the fire.) In your examination you found nothing—noth-
ing unusual?
　　DOCTOR. Unusual? She has a few bruises here and there
as if she had been struck or beaten by something. I really
don't know. She didn't open up to me. *(Thoughtfully.)*
It's peculiar though—
　　PRIEST. *(Crossing to bedroom door)* What's peculiar?
　　DOCTOR. The way she knew you were coming.

PRIEST. I'm going in to see her. *(He moves one step to the door.)*

DOCTOR. *(Restraining him)* Now, Father O'Malley, she's hysterical. She's in no mood for receiving visitors. *(To Center.)*

PRIEST. I'm not going without seeing her.

DOCTOR. But she doesn't want to see you. You'll only upset her further.

PRIEST. *(Crossing to above table)* Doctor Moran, have you ever heard of obsession?

DOCTOR. Obsession? Obsession about what?

PRIEST. You're a peculiar man, Doctor. You spend your days and your nights looking after the people of these wild bogs and islands and yet, like all doctors, you never look further than the poor, sick body you're trying to heal. *(Going to the door Left)* Bring her in. I want to have a word with her.

(Enter MICHAEL MARTIN *as* DOCTOR *goes to fireplace.)*

MICHAEL. *(In surly mood.)* She isn't well. She doesn't want to see you. She says the priest coming upset her.

PRIEST. Bring her in, all the same.

MICHAEL. *(At the door, roughly.)* Come on in out of that. He wants to have a word with you. Besides, we don't owe anything to anyone. *(To* MARY KATE, *who is off.)* Bring her in, you. Drag her in if she doesn't come quiet. *(Breaks to above door.)*

(Enter MARY KATE *leading* NORA *by the arm.* NORA *is blabbering and is in terror of the* PRIEST.)*

MARY. Come on in, alannah. Sure, no harm can come to you.

*(*NORA *breaks away from her and throws herself, cowering, on bench in front of the fireplace.)*

*(*MARY KATE *moves towards the* PRIEST. *With trust.)*
Father!

PRIEST. *(With sympathy.)* My poor woman!

MICHAEL. *(Crosses to* NORA, *pulling her up by her shoulders.)* Hold up your head. Where's your pride.

MARY. *(Pulling* MICHAEL MARTIN *back. Apologetic.)* Father, it's the way she's been turning himself and Patrick against everything holy. So you must forgive him if he's a bit rough.

PRIEST. *(Crossing to* NORA, *Left)* I understand. *(To* NORA.) You're welcome home, Nora. You mustn't be afraid. I've been told all about you and I've come to help you.

NORA. *(Moans and pants and watches him, in mortal agony.)* Go away. *(Hoarsely.)* Go away. I want to be left in peace.

DOCTOR. Now, Father, I warned you.

NORA. *(Runs across to Right.)* If he doesn't leave me alone I'll not be responsible for what will happen. I'll do something violent. *(Leaning on Right Center chair)* I'll tear down the house on top of the lot of you. *(Throws chair at cabinet.)*

MARY. She's mad.

PRIEST. Yes—mad—in a very peculiar way. *(He approaches* NORA *with his eyes fixed on hers. He speaks to her with great intensity.)* I am not afraid of you— *(Making the sign of the cross)* In nomine Patris et Filii et Spiritus Sancti— *(He places his hand on her head.)*
     (She wilts.)
(He lifts her by the arms.) Come with me. *(He leads her to a chair Center, where she sits. He still speaks intensely.)* Nora Geraty, I am not afraid of you— Do you hear me? *He crosses to Right of table.)*

(MARY KATE *and* MICHAEL MARTIN *move in.)*

NORA. *(Of a sudden she is composed.)* I hear you.

PRIEST. *(In front of table. On stool.)* Do you know who I am?

NORA. *(In a monotone.)* You are Father O'Malley from the foot of the mountain. I have known you since I was a child. You heard my first confession and gave me my first Holy Communion.

PRIEST. You know that I am your friend?

NORA. You are the friend of everyone, rich and poor.

PRIEST. You are at home amongst friends. Your father and mother are here beside you.

NORA. And my brother, Patrick. And Anthony Costello was here. He wanted to marry me before I went away. *(Displaying slight emotion)* And I wanted to marry him. I always wanted to marry him. But his farm was whines and rocks, as poor as my father's. So I thought I'd rise above the poverty of the rocky fields and I went to England.

PRIEST. You went to London. You worked in a factory and took lodgings in a house in Whitechapel.

NORA. You know everything. Father Richardson wrote to you.

PRIEST. How do you know he wrote to me?

(She makes no reply.)

You were introduced to spiritualism and used as a medium.

NORA. They said I was a simple girl and would be of use to them. When the day's work was over I'd come home and they'd start. La Cardami used to speak through me. She was a gypsy in Spain two hundred years ago. After a while I got frightened and wouldn't do it any more. And then it happened—

PRIEST. Yes?

NORA. One night in bed I dreamt that bombs were falling. The bricks of the house, the roof and the tiles were scattering in pieces about me. I wakened up in terror to find there was no raid but the room was full of the noise of banging and rapping on the wall. I put on the light but there was no one there.

MARY. *(Kneels.)* May God and His holy mother protect us.

MICHAEL. What is all that she's saying? What happened her in England? Why doesn't she talk so we could understand her?

DOCTOR. *(At Right.)* You're hypnotising the girl. And

terrifying her mother. You've no right to play about with the emotions of simple people like these.

PRIEST. I am not playing with their emotions as you say. I love my people. I love the people of this house. I'd sooner the evil had fallen on my head than on theirs. But they've got to learn the facts sooner or later and it's better for them to learn of it when you and I are here—better for their sanity.

(PATRICK *enters.*)

(To NORA.) Were these noises repeated?

NORA. Not for some time. But when it happened again it was much worse and I became terrified and ran away. But no matter where I went they were always there. *She* was always there. And then she began to strike me and beat me and people wondered at the marks.

MARY. *(Weeping)* Nora, Nora, what curse has come over you and over the lot of us?

PATRICK. What trumpery is going on here? *(To* PRIEST *and the* DOCTOR.) What trickery are the two of you up to?

MARY. Patrick, you're out of your senses.

(There is an exchange of looks.)

PRIEST. It's what I feared. *(To* PATRICK.) Patrick, you must never speak like that to your priest.

PATRICK. I'll speak just as I want to.

PRIEST. *(Witching* PATRICK *intently)* Now, I'm warning you to be careful of what you say.

PATRICK. I'll have no sister of mine mishandled and her good name dragged in the mud by anyone, be he priest or layman.

MARY. *(Crossing to him)* Sure the priest is as fond of Nora as you are and is only anxious to get her well.

PATRICK. Let him not think he'll put the fear of God on me with his threats. Thank heavens I got over that long ago.

MARY. *(To the* PRIEST.) I never knew him to be like that before. *(To* MICHAEL MARTIN.) Michael Martin, what sort of a man are you to allow your son to abuse the priest?

MICHAEL. I'll not interfere with anything he says or does. *((Walking away)* He's a mind of his own.

PRIEST. *(To* MARY KATE.*)* They're not responsible for what they're saying. Now, you'd do me a great favour if you and your husband and son left the doctor and myself alone for a while. *(Crosses down Right.)*

MARY. And will we leave Nora with you?

DOCTOR. *(Leans in.)* She seems to be in some kind of a daze or a trance. Take her over to the bed there.

(MICHAEL MARTIN *and* MARY KATE *take* NORA *to the bed, where she lies down.)*

MARY. *(As they move to the bed.)* Light the candle, Patrick.

(PATRICK *lights a candle at the fire.)*

Come on, Michael Martin. Come on, Patrick. These are men of schooling and know best what's to be done.

(Exit MARY KATE, MICHAEL MARTIN *to bedroom.* PRIEST *to bed, looks at* NORA.*)*

DOCTOR. Wait.

(PATRICK *exits Left with candle.)*

(DOCTOR *crosses in a bit.)* Now, now, Father O'Malley, what's all this high-falutin' business about?

PRIEST. *(Thoughtfully.)* Something is happening to this family—something it will take all my strength to fight.

DOCTOR. Bedad, you sound very mysterious.

PRIEST. Doctor Moran, I'm not a man given to wild flights of imagination. Life for me has always been a very hard affair indeed—reared on eight acres of rock on the edge of the Atlantic and graduating through a seminary where self-denial and mortification were the order of the day. I've disciplined myself to fear nothing. I have my imagination well under control. Yet, when I crossed the

threshold of this house I felt the beginnings of a fear such
as I have never experienced before.

DOCTOR. Fear! Fear of what? What is there to fear in a
four-walled cabin on the side of Coagh Patrick—bare
rocks outside and a pair of high-spirited, Connemara men
within? Aren't you an able-bodied man like myself?

PRIEST. *(Takes stage.)* My fear is not of things of this
world. There is something evil in this house. It's batter-
ing its way into the souls of the people who live in it. I'll
come to the point. Some time ago I had a letter from a
priest in England. He told me that he had come across
this young girl in a hospital over there and that he was
strongly of the opinion that she was the victim of obsession
—attacks, do you hear?—from without—by *evil spirits.*

DOCTOR. *(Blustering)* The girl's run-down. Her system
wants toning-up. Plenty of food and fresh air. There's
nothing complex in her case that I can see. *(Crosses to
Left below bed.)*

PRIEST. Father Richardson's theory is that she is being
periodically attacked by some evil agency she made contact with as a medium in England.

DOCTOR. *(Crossing to chair Right of table)* No sane
man will allow himself to be taken in by spiritualism. You
don't mean to tell me you see anything in it?

PRIEST. While admitting that it's a science that attracts
to itself many charlatans, I believe that such contacts are
possible.

DOCTOR. You amaze me. *(Going to the bed and examining* NORA'S *arm which lies exposed)* These are ordinary
bruises. I'm sure we'll find an explanation for them yet,
some very natural explanation.

PRIEST. I suppose you'll tell me next you don't believe
in the stigmata of Teresa Neumann? *(Crosses to Center.)*

DOCTOR. Now, Father O'Malley, I know little about
psychic matters. My business in life is to cure Pat
Murphy's pains and aches and to bring easy labour to Pat
Murphy's wife. But, out of the dim and distant past,
something vague comes to my mind about faith-healing
and auto-suggestion and the strange things they can do

to the body—like the stigmata you mentioned just now. And I can tell you this: if you think I'm going to sacrifice medicine to spiritual healing you're very much mistaken.

PRIEST. I have no intention of interfering with your treatment. But you must not interfere with mine.

DOCTOR. I hope I don't have to. *(Crosses to fireplace.)*

PRIEST. *(Right of bed. Watches* DOCTOR.) My treatment may have to deal with more than attacks from without, for obsession is frequently the forerunner of possession.

DOCTOR. You remind me of my old mother, God rest her soul, who firmly believed that Saint Patrick drove the devils from the summit of this mountain by ringing his famous bell.

PRIEST. *(Thoughtfully.)* Maybe he did. Maybe he did ring his bell and drive the Legion into the sea.

DOCTOR. *(Sits on bench.)* And the whole Christian world believed that Joshua commanded the sun to stand still until Galileo came along to prove that the earth moved round the sun. The point I am trying to make is this: that what seems obscure, inexplicable, supernatural today may tomorrow be explained by purely natural causes.

PRIEST. *(Crossing to above table)* The reality of possession is vouched for by Christ himself. He gave power to His followers to expel evil spirits in His name, and the Church has continued to use this power without interruption to the present day. History records many examples of possession and these records are in many cases compiled by non-Catholic writers.

DOCTOR. *(Rises.)* I imagine it could all be explained away by epilepsy or plain lunacy or this newfangled thing they talk about—schizophrenia. *(Crosses up to bed.)*

PRIEST. Are you questioning the divine inspiration of the Bible?

DOCTOR. I'm not saying that I do or I don't, but you can't blame me if I interpret what I read in a reasonable way. I'm a plain, logical fellow who looks for a reason in everything. I'm as good a Christian as you'll find in the

Barony of Murrisk. I say my prayers every night and I do my duty by my fellowman, but there's some Bible stories you'll never make me believe, like the very tall one of Lot's wife being turned into a pillar of salt.

PRIEST. You're a good-living man, Doctor, but I'd say that your acquaintance with theology doesn't go much farther than the Child's Penny Catechism. *(Up Center and opens door.)*

(Enter ANTHONY. *He is disturbed and anxious.)*

ANTHONY. Good night, Father.

PRIEST. Oh Anthony! Come in.

ANTHONY. Good night, Doctor. I heard the cars passing by our place and coming up here and I thought someone must be sick. Is it Nora?

*(*PRIEST *nods.)*

*(*ANTHONY *enters, closing the door behind him. He sees* NORA *on the bed.)* What's the matter with her?

PRIEST. *(Takes him to chair Center.)* Don't waken her. She's asleep.

ANTHONY. Where's the others?

PRIEST. They're inside. Come here, son. Nora and you used to be very friendly. *(Sits on bench at fire.)*

ANTHONY. We were, Father. More than friendly. I'm terrible fond of her. I was always fond of her. I might say she's more to me than my own flesh and blood, the farm and everything I own.

PRIEST. Well, son, there are some things that are hard to explain to a straightforward, young fellow like yourself. Nora isn't well.

ANTHONY. She looked bad when she arrived.

PRIEST. I am not attempting to explain to you the nature of her illness. All I ask of you is to trust me. I've been your confessor since you were a youngster of seven. You're a simple, honest, young man. You're fond of this girl. Your simplicity of heart and your fondness for her may yet be a great weapon against the powers of dark-

ness—if you are on my side. Anthony, I want you to trust
—I want you to have faith in me.

ANTHONY. *(Simply.)* Father, I trust you.

(FATHER O'MALLEY *goes slowly to the top of the bed and
looks at* NORA *for a few moments.* NORA *opens her
eyes.)*

NORA. *(Moans.)* Why am I troubled like this? You
must go away. You are against everything I do. I fear
you like death itself.

ANTHONY. Nora, you're in a dream. Wake up.

NORA. *(Mockingly)* Haec quotiescunque feceritis in
mei memoriam facietis.

ANTHONY. *(Going to foot of bed)* It's me—Anthony. I
don't understand what you're saying.

PRIEST. Lead her from the bed. Bring her to that chair
there.

(ANTHONY *takes her by the hand to chair below table
Left.* FATHER O'MALLEY *retires to the Center door.*
NORA *sits.)*

NORA. *(Mockingly)* In amnem terram exivit sonus
eorum et in fines orbis terrae verba eorum.

(The PRIEST *takes the holy-water font from the wall
and places it on the table behind* NORA. *She does not
see him.)*

Take it away. Take it away from me.

ANTHONY. But it's only the holy-water font.

NORA. It burns me. It burns me. It burns me. Don't let
it touch me. I hate it. *(She falls to the ground, cowering.)*

(The PRIEST *removes the font.)*

ANTHONY. *(Kneeling beside her and holding her hand)*
Nora, Nora, these are terrible things you're saying. Do
you know who I am? I'm Anthony Costello. I'm your
friend. We're all your friends here. We're going to help

you to get well. *(He lifts her to the chair. She becomes quite still. He kneels again.)*

PRIEST. The first sign of possession is the speaking fluently of a language which the energumen has never learned.

NORA. *(With rising agitation.)* He said in the letter "I have had her under observation for the past six months and it is my considered opinion that she is obsessed." Ha, ha, ha! *(She rises and approaches the* PRIEST *up Left. She speaks in the shrill voice of La Cardami.)* I was a Gitana in Spain. La Cardami they called me. I was a Moor before that and before that again I was in Egypt and the tombs. The others will soon be with me. *(She wails in eerie, Moorish melody the verse of a Romany song. She crosses down Center.)*

> "En los sastos de yesque plai me diquelo,
> Doscusanas de sonacai terelo
> Corojai diquelo abillar,
> Y ne asislo chapescar, chapescar."

ANTHONY. *(Right of her.)* Father, you didn't tell me it was like this.

(The PRIEST *signals to him to go to her again. Kneeling and kissing her hand)*

Nora, look at me— Look at me, Nora—

*(*NORA *looks blankly at him. He waves his hand before his eyes as if to drive away some strange influence which comes from her.)*

It's not you that's looking at me at all. Come out of the darkness. Come into the light. *I want you to listen to me—* You must not say—these queer things— I don't understand them— What are you trying to do to me? *(He pulls slightly away from her.)*

NORA. *(Drawing him towards her and holding him with her eyes)* Anthony— You love me— *(Leans into* ANTHONY. *Seductively.)* —Don't you?—

ANTHONY. *(Under her spell.)* —I love you—

NORA. Then why don't you kiss me?

ANTHONY. *(Suddenly draws away from her.)* I love you—but— *(He looks at the* PRIEST.)*

(The PRIEST *signals to him to go to* NORA *again.)*

You must listen to me. You must rest. No one here means
to do you any harm.

NORA. *(Frustrated.)* He is trying to harm me. But I
know all about him. I know the sins of his childhood. I
know all your sins. I'll tell them in the houses. I'll shout
them on the roads. I'll screech them on the shore. Yo le
conozco. Se educo et el Seminario de Salamanca, luego se
fue a Borneo y despuie a Nigeria y nos echo de los pos-
seidos. Vero le conquistamos. Se puso enfermo ye se le
mandaro en a casa. *(To* PRIEST.) He is a holy man and
he will try to exorcise me. With his prayers he will try to
conquer me. But I am strong. And I shall be stronger
when Beelzebub is here. *(With a despairing cry.)* Why
must I be oppressed like this? Why must you all torment
me? I want to be left in peace. *(She throws herself on
chair Right of table Left and weeps fitfully with her head
resting on her arms on the table. Then she subsides and
remains quite still.)*

PRIEST. Doctor Moran, are you convinced?

DOCTOR. *(At bed.)* The girl should be sent away to a
psychiatrist for observation. Who are you and I that we
should attempt to treat an unusual case like this?

PRIEST. There are none so blind as those that will not
see. *(Going to the door Left and opening it)* You may
come in now.

(Enter MARY KATE *followed by* MICHAEL MARTIN *and*
PATRICK.)

MARY. We didn't know you were here, Anthony.

ANTHONY. Father, what is it?

MARY. Father, what is it?

PRIEST. You must steel yourselves for what I'm about
to tell you.

MARY. Whatever it is we'd rather know. We're distracted ever since we got the letters.

PRIEST. Mrs. Geraty, have you ever heard of a person
being possessed of the devil?

MARY. *(With a gasp.)* Oh! Possessed! Possessed of the devil! You mean—that our daughter—

PRIEST. I have arrived at that conclusion only after mature consideration.

MARY. Oh, may God watch over us this night! *(To* MICHAEL MARTIN.) Did you hear what the priest said? I'd sooner she was dead. I'd sooner, a thousand times, she was in her grave.

MICHAEL. That's a queer thing for him to say. People shouldn't say things like that without being sure. How do we know it's true?

DOCTOR. *(Crossing to* FAMILY) I have told Father O'Malley that I am not in agreement with him. Until such time as we have been advised by people competent to deal with such extraordinary cases it is my duty to warn you against any interference with the girl—interference which will only aggravate her condition. Her nerves are completely upset and religious fanaticism may easily land her in the madhouse. *(He takes his bag and exits Center.)*

MICHAEL. The doctor is a man of learning too. Why shouldn't his word be taken as well as the next?

PRIEST. *(To* MICHAEL MARTIN.) I am going to see the Bishop tomorrow to discuss this case with him. If he agrees that exorcism is necessary I shall have to apply formally to her family for permission to go ahead with the rite of driving the spirit out of her. I hope I shall meet with no opposition from you. Do you understand what I'm saying?

(MICHAEL MARTIN *walks away and sits by the fire.)*

MARY. We understand you, Father. And we have faith in you. We'll leave everything in your hands. We know you'll cure her.

PRIEST. *(Pause.)* In the meantime, I commend you to pray and to pray especially that the evil which has possessed your daughter does not communicate itself to her father and her brother. *(He looks at* MICHAEL MARTIN

*and makes the sign of the cross in the air. He takes his
hat, coat and bag and exits Center.)*

(NORA *opens her eyes, darts to the door, opens it and
looks out into the darkness after the priest. She faces
about, looks savagely around the kitchen, puts her
hand over her eyes and leans against the door which
closes behind her. She takes her hand away, opens her
eyes and looks in surprised fashion at the* OTHERS,
*who are watching her intently. She is again normal.
With a cry of "Mother," she runs to her mother's
arms.)*

CURTAIN

(End of Act Two.)

ACT THREE

The scene is the same. It is Sunday morning, a few weeks later. the day of the annual pilgrimage to Croagh Patrick. The picture of the Sacred Heart and the holy-water font are missing. MICHAEL MARTIN *and* MARY KATE, *having returned from the pilgrimage, are finishing breakfast.* MICHAEL MARTIN *is dressed in Sunday best with frieze coat and trousers, white front and heavy boots.* MARY KATE *also wears heavy boots, a blouse and skirt. Her shawl lies thrown over the back of a chair.* PATRICK *leans against the door jamb, smoking a cigarette. He is looking up towards the mountain. There is a drifting mist outside.*

MICHAEL. *(Crosses to door Center.)* Is there any sign of her yet?

PATRICK. I can't see anything with the mist—it's that heavy. A minute ago it cleared away and I could see the crowds thick on the summit around the chapel. But no sign of her at all. *(He cups his hands and calls out into the fog.)* Nora—

MICHAEL. *(To* PATRICK.) Didn't I tell you not to let her out of your sight for an instant? That's why we left her here with you while we went to the pilgrimage.

PATRICK. I was in the house with her all the time. Then I left to feed the calf and when I came back she was gone. If the mist wasn't coming that thick in my face from the sea I might have seen what way she went. *(Comes in.)*

MARY. She'll find her way, don't you fret. That girl knows every hole and corner on the mountain.

PATRICK. *(Calling into the fog)* Nora—Nora—

MICHAEL. *(Crossing to table Left)* She'll be starved too with nothing on her stomach.

MARY. Father O'Malley said she was to fast and pray.

58

So, don't get on to her again about eating. Please God, after today everything will be all right.

(PATRICK takes his cap from the top of the cabinet and exits to the yard.)

MICHAEL. *(Crossing to door. Shouting after him)* Don't you go too far. You better be here when the priest comes. He said everyone was to be in the house today. *(Crossing back to table. To MARY KATE.)* It'd be like him to slip away when he knows I want him here beside me. I hope Willie the Post comes soon.

MARY. He better. *(Takes teapot to fireplace.)* For if the priest finds him at that game again he'll read him off the altar. I wouldn't have him near the place at all only for yourself and to be at peace with you—especially the day that's in it. But I'll not have him doing the Marthainn in front of Nora. 'Twould only upset her further.

MICHAEL. You better find some way of getting her out of the house then before Willie comes.

(The DOG is heard outside, barking.)

Sh!—

(They listen for a moment. MARY KATE goes to the door and peers into the fog. The DOG barks again. MICHAEL MARTIN now goes to the door and stands outside with MARY KATE, looking towards the mountain. The fog swirls around them and then lightens. After a few moments NORA appears. BOTH regard her curiously and then MARY KATE leads her in. MICHAEL MARTIN follows. NORA wears a small shawl around her head.)

MARY. Are you all right, agradh?

NORA. *(Crossing to fireplace)* I'm all right, Mother. *(She takes off her shawl and heaves it aside.)*

MARY. We were worrying about you. The mist came that thick.

NORA. There was no need to be upset.

MICHAEL. *(Crossing to NORA)* How were we to know

you didn't lose your way and fall down the front of the mountain side? Did you have anything to eat?

NORA. I'll just have a cupful of milk. *(Crossing to chair Right of table.)*

(MARY KATE *fills a cup with milk and gives it to* NORA. MICHAEL MARTIN *puts on his hat and goes to the door Center.)*

MICHAEL. *(Awkwardly. Pacing)* You should try and eat up something—a plate of stirabout—or if you beat her up a raw egg. *(He exits.)*

MARY. He's a queer man is Michael Martin Geraty.

NORA. *(Drinking milk)* Was there a great crowd at the pilgrimage?

MARY. Near as big as ever it was. The Bishop himself was there. The poor man is getting very feeble. He had to travel near all the way up on a pony.

NORA. I saw no one at all climbing from this side.

MARY. Ah, sure, Nora, they haven't done that for years. The Killsallagh people likes to go to Murrisk now and climb with them coming from the towns. The time I married your father there'd be crowds and crowds passing by that door there, some of them going up and more coming down on their way to Kilgeever to finish the pilgrimage at the Blessed Well.

NORA. The morning is long passing.

MARY. *(Gives her dishpan.)* Let you do a few things now to keep yourself busy. The doctor said it was better for you to be busy and not to be moping all the time. Tidy up the table and then you might give me a hand feeding the hens.

(NORA *clears the table.* MARY KATE *breaks up potatoes with her hands in a basin and adds meal from a sack which stands on a chair and hot water from a kettle on the fire.)*

MARY. The way it is—no matter what the trouble, the

work has to be done. The hens has to be fed. The cattle must be looked after, the sheep driven down from the mountain. Whenever your brothers and sisters went away I found comfort in hard work and little time for crying.

NORA. *(Starts washing dishes.)* I know all that, Mother, and you can't deny that I've done my best not to be a nuisance. God knows, I've been fighting against my fear and depression, day and night. But, just this morning, I can't keep my mind off it. *(Stops washing.)* What will they do to me when they come?

MARY. *(Crossing in above table)* I know no more than you do. There'll be the nuns from the convent in Louisburg and the family will be here in the kitchen. And on this holy morning, with your own flesh and blood beside you, you'll have nothing to fear.

NORA. Even Father O'Malley won't tell what's going to happen. I sometimes wonder whether Doctor Moran isn't right after all and I should go away for examination. *(Resumes washing.)*

MARY. I've warned you already against that way of thinking. Haven't I trouble enough with your father and brother?

NORA. I seem to get upset more often. Things happen a lot now, don't they? In the last few days, I mean.

MARY. Now, there you go again, talking about yourself all the time.

NORA. What happened last night? When I wakened up you were all standing about and Dad was crying.

MARY. It was nothing much. Himself was a bit upset because you were the only daughter left to us. What he said was he was sorry he was rough with you the night you came back.

NORA. I know now so well when it's coming on. I get a tightening in my throat and my breath catches me here and I begin to choke.

MARY. Now, now, have you not them things washed up yet?

NORA. It's the waiting for it to happen—that's what I can't bear. And it's happening oftener now. Isn't it? Isn't it? *(Crosses to MARY.)*

MARY. You're upsetting me. You should pray at the very first sign.

NORA. I don't know about prayer— It doesn't seem to help any more. And then this thing about himself and Patrick—they're turning terrible against the priest. I know it's my doing.

MARY. You must have faith in God and His holy mother. Father O'Malley said that faith would move even the mountains themselves. *(Crosses up to door.)*

NORA. It's hard to pray when you're sick. *(She goes to the door and throws the dirty water on the flags outside. She then stands looking into the distance.)* There's a queer stillness about the morning. The mist is drifting away and the sea is that grey it's like the grey sky itself spread out before you. It's a lonesome country—very lonesome— *(Crosses down to table.)*

MARY. 'Tis the rain in the air. 'Tis always quiet like that before the rain. Now, when you're finished washing up you can tidy the bedroom or come out and give me a hand with the fowl. There's plenty of work to be done. *(She exits to the yard with the basin of feeding.)*

(NORA has by now dried the dishes which she starts to place on the cabinet. At the cabinet she stops and looks thoughtfully at the shelf where the statue used to be and comes back to the table for more delph. She hangs them on the cabinet and looks at the spot on the wall where the picture of the Sacred Heart used to hang. She goes to it, hesitatingly touches the spot and moves her hand over it. She draws quickly back and goes down on her knees at the table.)

NORA. Mother of God, don't let it come on me again. I believe in God. *(In a hoarse whisper.)* I believe in God. I believe in God.

(ANTHONY *appears at the Center door. The crisis leaves* NORA.)

ANTHONY. I'm disturbing you at your prayers.

NORA. *(Running to him and throwing her arms about him)* Oh, Anthony, I'm so glad you came. I was terrified.

ANTHONY. Now, what have you to be terrified of? This is a nice hour of the day to be praying! *(Lightly.)* Next thing we'll hear you'll be entering the convent and taking the veil! Sister Nora Geraty, if you don't mind!

NORA. 'Twas the hand of God sent you. *(Sits at table.)* When you're around I'm strong. There's something about you drives away this awful fear.

ANTHONY. *(Lifts her up.)* Isn't it time you got rid of them pale cheeks and that scared look? You mustn't be scared. Do you hear me?

NORA. *(Crossing to up Center)* I'm scared of everything—of this evil thing that hangs over me. And I'm scared for Patrick and himself. They wouldn't let the priest near the house at all only herself stood up strong against them and said she'd be master for this once. And I'm scared I'll lose you—that I'll not get well and you'll leave me.

ANTHONY. I'll never leave you.

NORA. You'll stay when they come, won't you?

ANTHONY. Of course I'll stay.

NORA. *(Points to walls.)* They've taken away the picture—and all the pictures in the rooms—the picture of the Sacred Heart—do you remember? You see, they're afraid of me. I can see it when they look at me.

ANTHONY. *(Crossing to above table)* Now, I had a long chat with Father O'Malley last night. He told me to come up first thing in the morning to see you. He said I was to talk to you and to tell you that you must believe in the goodness of God and have faith in Him.

NORA. You're a good boy, Anthony.

ANTHONY. *(Sits above table.)* Yerra, I'm not. But I believe in doing what I was reared to do—not because I think the old people are always right—but prayers and

religion make you content and happy and keep you out
of harm's way.

NORA. Oh, Anthony! Anthony! *(She is smiling.)* You'd
make a lovely priest.

ANTHONY. Go on out of that with you, you codger you!
But we must be afraid of nothing—either of us. Do you
know, this morning I feel I could lift Croagh Patrick out
of the bowels of the earth and carry it to Louisburg on my
shoulders. I'll soon have you the girl you used to be—
full of divilment and fun. *(Rising)* Go on. Smile for me
again.

NORA. You're like a warm wind to me—a soft, warm
wind in April.

ANTHONY. *(Sits on table.)* Say, who's doing the love-
making, you or me? Plastering up to me like you used to
in the old days!

NORA. Don't tell me you didn't like it. There's no man
living doesn't like a bit of plastering now and then.

ANTHONY. Yes, always playing ducks and drakes with
me—flying up and down the mountain like a colt with a
black mane streaming behind you, impudent and bold,
and putting the comehither on every man in Killsallagh
and on me in particular. And then when you had me nicely
spancelled, off you went and left me in the lurch.

NORA. I'm afraid we were a wild lot up here. The Taobh
na Cruaiche goats they always called us.

ANTHONY. Do you remember the night your bike broke
down coming from the dance at Bunowen?

NORA. And we arrived home at six o'clock in the morning in the streels of rain! And himself skelped hell out of
me!

ANTHONY. Do you remember Johnny McBride's wedding when we all went to the fair at Murrisk and Johnny
got so drunk he fell in a boat and wakened up all by
himself in the morning?

NORA. And everyone thought he ran away and Katie
went home crying and had to spend the night with her
mother! I wasn't a bit sorry for her. There was no standing
her after she hooked Johnny McBride.

ANTHONY. Go on. You're jealous. Jealous because poor Katie's married.

NORA. *(Rises.)* Jealous! I'm never jealous. I don't care if I was never married. *(Crosses to settle up Right.)*

ANTHONY. Liar!

NORA. *(Sits on settle.)* But Katie's wedding was a yell, wasn't it? Do you remember when they found Johnny they couldn't get him out of the boat because he was jammed between the seats!

ANTHONY. *(Crossing to settle.)* That's good. I have you laughing again. Ah, we had great fun in the old days. *(Embraces her.)* I love you— I love you.

MARY. *(Enters carrying a jug of water.)* Is this who you have with you now?

NORA. We were talking about old times. Anthony actually made me laugh.

ANTHONY. Ah, I was only doing my best to cheer her up.

MARY. Why don't you take her out for a walk to the brow of the hill? She'll get a breath of air from Connemara will do her more good than all the medicines in the world.

ANTHONY. Come on. 'Twill put new life in you. We'll clear over the rock like a pair of mountain goats.

NORA. You must be here when they come.

MARY. Now, you won't be far away and we can shout after you. Off with the pair of you!

(Exit NORA and ANTHONY Center, hand in hand. MARY KATE looks after them and then pours water from the jug which she carries into a pot on the fire. She goes to the door, looks after ANTHONY and NORA and waves to someone in the opposite direction. WILLIE THE POST and MICHAEL MARTIN appear.)

MICHAEL. Where are they gone to?

MARY. For a walk to the brow of the hill.

MICHAEL. Come in quick, Willie. We never know when Father O'Malley might be here.

(WILLIE *and* MICHAEL MARTIN *enter.* WILLIE *takes a cloth parcel from his bag and opens it on the table Left.)*

WILLIE. Did you get the water from the stream?

MARY. *(At fire.)* I have it on the fire boiling.

WILLIE. Now, I hope you didn't take it against the stream. 'Twould be no use at all if you did.

MICHAEL. She took it with the running as you told her.

WILLIE. *(Dramatically.)* I have everything here—seven handfuls of meal, seven pieces of garlic and seven coals taken from the bonfire on the Eve of Saint John. And curse the robbers in Louisburg that threw stones and shouted at me as I drew coals from the bonfire in the square of the town! May they never prosper! And a feather from the tail of the Michaelmas goose for luck! *(He produces a goose quill.)* When the water boils we'll put everything in. And here's a bit of Ealabhuidh I plucked on the third Friday following the Eve of Saint Martin's next November a year gone. If you get her to wear it around her neck, 'twill keep all evil away.

MICHAEL. She be's a queer, obstinate girl at times. But we'll do our best. *(Crosses to* MARY KATE; *gives her quill.)* You might try hanging it over her bed at night. 'Tis at night we be most upset.

WILLIE. How is she now?

MICHAEL. You can hardly get a word out of her at all —or a laugh—her that used to be so bright. She be's that quiet you'd wonder what she's thinking about. And she's getting worse. I know it in my heart and soul. And the fits come on her more and more. I wonder if that priest is doing her any good. That's why I sent for you to do the Marthainn.

WILLIE. Have anything new happened since himself came to me?

MARY. Last night she was that bad we tried to hold her down in the bed but she had the strength of seven horses. And then, Willie, God between us and all harm, something that none of us could see lifted her clean out of the bed into the air. There's things happened in this house since the night she came back I'm afraid to tell anyone about.

WILLIE. 'Twas the evil eye was put on her. She's enchanted. It might be when she was only a child. There was a woman called Ward had the evil eye. A tinker woman she was—red-headed. Not a cow in Pat Philbin's gave milk for years where Pat said something to her on the road, of a fair day he was drunk.

MARY. The doctor fears she'll go mad but the priest says no—'tis a power from another world.

MICHAEL. People sometimes has too much faith in the priest. If I had my way I'd never let him darken the door. Every time he comes near her the fit comes on again.

WILLIE. 'Twas the evil eye, I tell you. May it burn in the fire of God! May it be plucked out by the roots and its light put out for ever! May the hand wither that brought this curse on the house!

MARY. He was to the Bishop and everything's fixed and he's to read the Gospel over her today. If she's not cured soon I think I'll go mad myself or die of fret.

WILLIE. *(Chanting quietly. Crossing to fire slowly)*
   "Uisg an Easain,
    Air mo dhosan,
    Tog dhiom do rosad,
    'S aghaidb fir cabbaig orm."

(Thus chanting he approaches the fire, holding parcel out in front of him.) The water is boiling. Kneel down. We'll say a Hail Mary.

   (They kneel down in front of the fire and murmur the Hail Mary in Irish.)

Get up now, let ye, and sit there by the fire. And not a stir out of ye, no matter what happens.

   (MARY KATE sits on one side of the fire. MICHAEL MARTIN stands, watching intently.)

(WILLIE puts parcel on the floor in front of the fire, sits on stool and puts handfuls of the mixture into the pot. He stirs the mixture with a three-branched stick. As he stirs the mixture.)

Claoidhtear seang; feart fial, Aine 'sa g-cill go buan,
Go buadh na gcraobh nglaise; sugh na geige geire, gile.
Go mbudh subhach suam mise agus ingean
Aonghuis Sail Ghlais,
Gidh nar budh ionann duinn run oreidimb.

Gan d'ar ngradh againn air am talamh acht Aine,
Beannacht leis an anam a bhi i gcorp Aine ni haille
Agus gach neach a mbeidh an Marthainn seo aige
      Beannacht dar ngradh-ne.

*(He rises and walks around the kitchen with his eyes half
shut and his arms stretched in front of him. In one hand
he holds the branched stick with which he makes the sign
of the cross on the door, on the furniture, on the threshold
and in the air.)*

Dia romhaim,
Muire an deaghaidh.
'Sam Mac a tug Ri na nDul,
'sa chairach Brigid na glaic.
Mis'air do shlios, a Dhia,
Is Dia na'm luirg.
Mac Muire, a's Ri na nDul,
A shoillseachadh gach ni dheth so,
Le a ghras, mu'm choinneamh.

*(He stops opposite the door Center and opens his eyes.
The mist again sweeps across the mountain. The
sound of curlews is heard.)*

MICHAEL. *(In a tense whisper.)* What do you see,
Willie? What do you see?

WILLIE. *(At door.)* Out there in the mist I see a bird
flying. A big, white bird. Flocks and flocks of birds on
the wing. Yes, birds flying is a good sign.

MICHAEL. What else?

WILLIE. There's something out there against the rocks.
—A kind of a queer, black shape— Yes, it's a beast lying
down in the field.

MICHAEL. Lying down!

WILLIE. Wait! Wait! 'Tis rising. A beast rising in the field is a sign she will recover.

MICHAEL. Good. Good.

WILLIE. But the best sign of all—a man is coming to the house!

PATRICK. *(Appears at the door.)* Ye better stop that. The priest is coming.

WILLIE. The priest! The Lord preserve us!

(WILLIE *quickly collects his cloth and stick and retires to one side.* PATRICK *has entered. The* PRIEST *now appears at the door. Behind him are two Sisters of Mercy—*MOTHER BENEDICT, *aged fifty-five, and* SISTER MARY *of the Rosary, aged thirty-five.)*

PRIEST. *(To* WILLIE.) What are you doing here?

(WILLIE *makes no reply.)*

(The PRIEST *sees the pot on the fire and takes in the situation. Wearily, crossing to fireplace.)* Haven't I enough to contend with without this pagan nonsense? *(To* MARY KATE.) I ask you to have faith and you turn to superstition. Must I be alone in the fight? *(To* WILLIE.) Go home, and never let me catch you at this tomfoolery again.

(WILLIE *slips out.)*

MARY. I'm sorry, Father. But it was how himself thought that maybe Willie could do some good. Sure I knew in my heart and soul he couldn't.

PRIEST. "Unless ye see signs and wonders ye believe not." *(To chair Right of table.)*

MARY. *(To the* NUNS.) Will you come in, Mam. Come in, Mam.

(Enter the NUNS.)

Sit down, Father. *(She dusts chair for him.)* Get chairs, will ye.

(This to MICHAEL MARTIN *and* PATRICK, *who get settle for the* NUNS.)

Ye'll excuse us if the kitchen is a bit upset but 'tis the way things are.

(NUNS sit on settle up Left Center. MARY KATE takes the pot from the fire and puts it on the hearth.)

PRIEST. Where is she?

MARY. Go round the back of the house, Patrick, and shout to them to come down. Or whistle the way they'll know we want them .
    (Exit PATRICK Center.)
She went out for a walk with Anthony Costello.

PRIEST. *(Crossing to MARY KATE)* I've brought Mother Benedict and Sister Mary of the Rosary. They taught Nora at the convent and knew her well.

BENEDICT. I prepared her for First Holy Communion, Mrs. Geraty, and Confirmation and Sister Mary of the Rosary taught her in fifth and sixth classes. She was always a good girl. Wasn't she, Sister?

ROSARY. Very nice. A very nice girl, indeed.

BENEDICT. A bit lively, perhaps, and with a mind of her own and not always responsive to our teachings. But which of us is perfect? The Lord himself says "The just man falls seven times a day."

MICHAEL. *(At Right Center.)* It doesn't do for women or young girls to have notions of their own. I tried my best to knock it out of her but, as the saying is, you can take a horse to the water but you can't make him drink.

BENEDICT. Of course, we knew her sisters well too. They were among our first pupils. Clever children they were and promising.

ROSARY. Very clever and very independent.

BENEDICT. But good at attendance.

ROSARY. Oh, very good indeed, Reverend Mother.

MICHAEL. I saw that they went, hail, rain or snow.

MARY. Himself believed in giving them every chance of bettering themselves. They're all in America now, praise be to God, all married and settled down with families of their own.

BENEDICT. Isn't that nice?

ROSARY. Very nice indeed.

BENEDICT. Do they write?

MARY. Many's the letter we've had from them. And many's the time they talked of the nuns and how the learning they got stood to them in America. They never forgot you and all you did for them. I'm sure you found them a handful at times.

BENEDICT. *(Changing the subject)* Isn't this a very nice cottage, Sister?

ROSARY. Very nice indeed, Reverend Mother. Swept bare and clean by the high winds of heaven. Like the holy mountain itself.

BENEDICT. Very quaint and in the best style of peasant architecture. *(To* MARY KATE.) Sister Mary of the Rosary is from the country herself. Of course, I'm a city woman —Dublin. But Sister Mary of the Rosary is from the County Wexford.

MARY. Fancy now, coming that long way!

ROSARY. I was looking at the settle. It reminded me of home. Kilmore Quay I come from—yes—in the County Wexford. It's by the sea. The road runs down to the harbour and there are houses all the way—two-stories white houses with thatched roofs and gardens—a garden in front of every house and every house as white as snow— Very nice— Yes, very nice indeed.

MARY. Ah, you must be terrible lonesome for it.

BENEDICT. *(Again changing the subject.)* Will she be long, Mrs. Geraty?

MARY. She won't be a minute, Mam. Go out, Michael Martin, and see what's keeping them.

(Exit MICHAEL MARTIN *Center.)*

You're not to mind himself. He's upset. Father, I'm afraid of what will happen when she comes in. Wouldn't it be awful for the nuns if she—

PRIEST. I've told them all about her. They understand.

MARY. *(To the* REVEREND MOTHER.) It's a curse that's fallen on us, Mam. Isn't it? A terrible curse. I'm distracted. *(Sits above table.)*

BENEDICT. *(Crossing to* MARY*)* You must pray and have faith in God and His Holy mother. The prayers of the community are being offered for her, night and day. And she must have faith herself too. Without it she is lost.

ROSARY. Saint Benedict was all-powerful against evil spirits. Mother Benedict has great faith in her patron saint.

BENEDICT. I have brought you his medal. You must wear it.

(She gives MARY KATE *a medal which* MARY KATE *kisses and pins on her blouse.* MICHAEL MARTIN *and* PATRICK *enter.* PATRICK *goes to the fireplace and sits.* MICHAEL MARTIN *stands, looking moodily on.)*

Is this your son, Mrs. Geraty?

MARY. That's Patrick. Raise your cap, Patrick, to the nuns.

*(*PATRICK *removes his cap. The* PRIEST *moves into a corner up Left.)*

PATRICK. They're coming.

*(*ANTHONY *appears, holding* NORA'S *hand.* NUNS *rise.)*

ANTHONY. Come on, Nora.
NORA. You are here— I—
ANTHONY. They are here. Come in.

(They enter. ANTHONY *holds her by the arm.)*

MARY. The nuns is here—and the priest— They taught you at school. Won't you say you're glad to see them?

BENEDICT. Of course she's glad to see us. You remember Sister Mary of the Rosary, don't you?

NORA. *(Center.)* I could never forget her. She taught me the area of every country in Europe and never stopped calling me a harumscarum. But I'm thankful for all the patience she took with me and I'm grateful for her visit here today— *(Her voice trails away.)*

ROSARY. Mother Benedict and I are both very interested in you and welcome you home. You must come to the convent to see us. We are always glad of a visit from an old pupil.

MARY. Why don't you shake hands with them, Nora? You mustn't make strange with people coming to the house.

NORA. I'm not making strange at all. *(She advances to shake hands with them but stops suddenly.)*

ROSARY. *(Approaches her, holding an envelope.)* I've brought you some Agnus Dei. I made them myself. You must wear them.

NORA. It was very thoughtful—and nice of you—but somehow—when holy things— *(She takes the envelope but drops it at once.)* Anthony!

ANTHONY. Yes, Nora. I'm here.

NORA. I wish they hadn't— It would be better if they—went—away—

ANTHONY. Don't let yourself slip away again. Nora!

NORA. *(Waving him aside and changing character)* This is no social call. We all know why they are here. He told them I was possessed. Didn't he? Didn't he? He'll try to exorcise me. He'll tie me to the bed and say his prayers over me. *(Takes chair Right of table.)* But he'll fail for I am wiser than he is. You see, I am older—hundreds of years older. *(This is the voice of La Cardami. She laughs in the face of the PRIEST.)*

(MOTHER BENEDICT lifts her rosary beads and prays.)

ANTHONY. *(Tensely.)* Nora!

PRIEST. *(In a whisper.)* Sister, move away from her.

(But ROSARY is watching NORA, fascinated.)

BENEDICT. Sister Mary of the Rosary. *(With an urgent whisper. She touches the sister on the shoulder.)*

(ROSARY, with a start, moves away.)

NORA. He thinks he'll conquer me but I'll conquer him. I'll overwhelm him, body and soul. I'll tear the life from his body though he tie me to the bed like a beast. Will my family stand for this? *(This in her own voice.)* Have I no one to fight on my side? Where is my brother? Where is my brother Patrick?

PATRICK. *(Going to her)* I'm here. I'm on your side. I dare them to touch you. I dare them to try any of their tricks on you. *(He has taken a stand beside her.)*

PRIEST. It's the cunning hand of the devil.

PATRICK. There is no devil. There is no devil in her at all, I say. She's my sister and you're driving her mad with your superstition and your magic. But I'll not let ye touch a hair of her head. Clear out of the house, every manjack of you. If you don't I'll take her in my arms and carry her out of the house for ever.

PRIEST. Take care lest you too become a victim of this evil. Don't you see the demon is playing with you? It's one of his tricks. Take care lest he claim your immortal soul.

PATRICK. That's talk from the altar and carries no weight with me. *(To* MICHAEL MARTIN.*)* Are you going to stand there too and see your daughter made a fool of and the laughing-stock of the countryside? Are you her father at all, man, or only a clod of earth? Where's your pride?

MICHAEL. *(Taking his place beside* NORA *and* PATRICK*)* The boy is right. I should have put my foot down from the start.

(The PRIEST *moves towards them.)*

Don't attempt to come a step nearer. If you do I'll not be responsible for my actions.

(As the PRIEST *makes another move.)*

I'm telling you to stay where you are. And get out of the house, the lot of you, before I do something desperate.

PRIEST. I command you to leave the side of that girl— I command you to do what I say— Get away I tell you— Get away from her side at once— *(He makes the sign of the cross in the air.)* In nomine Patris et Filii et Spiritus Sancti—

(MICHAEL MARTIN *and* PATRICK *are stunned by the intensity of the* PRIEST'S *voice.* MICHAEL MARTIN *stands still.* PATRICK *runs to a chair up Right where he covers his face with his arm.)*

NORA. *(Beating her hands in rage against her father's breast)* Do not let him beat you. He's only a man like yourselves. I hate him. I hate his crucifixes and his statues. *(With arms outstretched, crosses to* PRIEST *Center.)* If I had the power I'd turn earth and heaven upside down, bring the stars crashing from the sky, let loose the fires from the bowels of the earth and have hell reign over all. I renounce God. *(Crosses to* NUNS.) I praise the devil and all his works and pomps—his works and his pomps—his works and his pomps—

MARY. Father for God's sake stop her—

NORA. *(Screeching)* Put him out or I'll kill him before the eyes of the lot of you. Put him out, I say. *(She rushes to claw* PRIEST *but* ANTHONY *quickly grasps her.)*

ANTHONY. Nora! Nora!

(She relaxes and collapses on her knees against AN-THONY *who supports her.)*

Father.

PRIEST. *(Approaching)* Stay where you are, Anthony—Nora Geraty—

NORA. *(Weakly.)* Yes, Father?

PRIEST. *(On one knee, with his hands on* NORA'S *shoulders.)* You are possessed, body and soul. If you can, let you pray and try to excite in yourself an active faith in God and His goodness and be resigned to His most holy will. You must not doubt. You must believe. Nora Geraty, *do you believe?*

NORA. *(In a weak voice.)* I believe.

PRIEST. Then may God in His mercy give me strength.

(MARY KATE makes a move to take her.)

Take her you, Anthony.

(ANTHONY *leads* NORA *to the bedroom.* MOTHER
BENEDICT *follows.* MARY KATE *goes to the door and
looks after them.* PATRICK *is seated on a chair with
his head sunk.* MICHAEL MARTIN *goes to the fire and
sits, looking gloomily into it. The* PRIEST *takes a
surplice, a violet stole, a crucifix and a copy of the
"Rituale Romanuum" from his bag. He vests himself
in the surplice and stole.* ROSARY *assists him and
lights a candle which she takes from the bag. The
candle is in a silver candlestick. To the* OTHERS.)
You may come into the room if you wish. If you prefer to
stay here I exhort you to pray—to pray more fervently
than you've ever prayed before—for your daughter—and
for me.

(Preceded by ROSARY, *who carries the candle, the* PRIEST,
*holding the crucifix aloft, goes to the door of the
bedroom, blesses himself and exits.* MARY KATE
*is upset and sits on chair Right of table. The Litany
of the Saints is heard. Then the noise of a CAR. They
look up but are too apathetic to rise. The* DOCTOR
enters.)

DOCTOR. Where is Father O'Malley?
MARY. He's inside in the room—
DOCTOR. *(Goes to the bedroom door and looks in.)* So,
he's started, bell, book and candle. *(Calling)* Father
O'Malley— *(There is no reply but the loud responses of
the Litany. The* DOCTOR *comes back into the kitchen and
looks at the Geraty family who are hardly aware of his
presence. To* MARY KATE.) I can't understand this blind
faith.
      (MARY KATE *does not reply.)*
If she were my daughter I'd sooner see her dead. Are you
sure the Bishop has been consulted? *(The* DOCTOR *goes
to* MICHAEL MARTIN.) I told you, Geraty, I was arrang-
ing to have her sent away You're a fool to allow yourself
to be browbeaten by the priest. Who gave him authority
to go ahead?

(MICHAEL MARTIN *looks dumbly at him.*)
You've no pride in you—no manhood. You're whipped. I'll take the matter into my own hands. *(He goes quickly to the bedroom door but stops, draws back and crosses himself as if he saw something frightful inside. He remains for a few moments looking into the room and moves fearfully into it. The Litany of the Saints is heard.)*

PRIEST. *(Off.)* Ne reminiscaris, Domine, delicta nostra, vel parentum nostrorum; neque vindictam sumas de peccatis nostris. Pater noster—

PATRICK. *(Jumping up)* I can't sit here.

MARY. Where are you going, son?

PATRICK. If I was doing something—driving the cattle —feeding the calves—anything at all. But I can't sit here, thinking and waiting.

MARY. You can pray.

PATRICK. I can't pray. What good would my prayers be?

MICHAEL. You better not leave the yard. You never can tell when we might be wanted.

(PATRICK *takes a bucket and exits Center to the yard.)*

MARY. He's no longer happy here. He'd be better away altogether, fending for himself.

MICHAEL. And what we do then? Who would there be to carry on the farm? He's a good boy. He's my son. I won't have anything said against him.

NORA. *(Loudly, off.)* Sacerdos est daemonium ipse. Sacerdos est Beelzebub.

MARY. *(Going to the bedroom door)* That's her again.

PRIEST. *(In a strong voice, off.)* Exorciso te, immundissime spiritus, omne plantasma, omnis legio, in nomine Domini nostri, Jesu Christi—

NORA. *(Off.)* Do not adjure me. Do not adjure me.

(MARY KATE *comes to the fire, kneels and says her rosary.* MICHAEL MARTIN *restlessly jumps up, goes to the bedroom door, looks in, moves wildly around the kitchen and goes back to the bedroom door.)*

MICHAEL. Who am I to be browbeat like this? I was a fool to let him into the house at all this day.

MARY. Kneel down and pray with me— Kneel down, I say.

MICHAEL. *(Not heeding her.)* The doctor is a wiser man than any priest. You heard what he said. He was for sending her to a hospital but you wouldn't let him. You said the priest fixed it all up between you. Ye'll drive her to the madhouse with your prayers.

PRIEST. *(Off.)* Ipse tibi imperat qui de te supernis caelorium in inferiora terrae demergi praecepit. Ipse tibe imperat—

MICHAEL. *(Rushing up to the Center door)* Where's that son of mine?

(As he opens the door PATRICK *appears with a bucket of water. Crosses to fireplace.)*

Come in. What do you mean being away so long? Didn't I tell you to stay here beside me?

*(*PATRICK *fills a pot with water from the bucket. He puts meal in the pot and hangs the pot on the fire. Both* PATRICK *and his father are restless.)*

When I give orders here they're to be obeyed. I'll be master in my own house for the future. I'll be no laughing-stock for the parish. Let the priest be boss in the chapel if he wants to but he has no right trying to rule the roost in another man's house.

PATRICK. *(At his business.)* That old dog is getting blind. It's time someone went over to Uncle Pat's for the dog he promised. That same Uncle Pat would promise you the sun, moon and stars but you'd have to travel for them yourself.

MICHAEL. *(Roughly.)* The dog can wait.

PATRICK. *(Roughly, in reply.)* Them sheep'll be strayed to Drummin if they're not brung down at once. *(Crosses to cabinet.)*

MICHAEL. I don't care if they're never brung down— My head is bothered. How come in such trouble to fall on this house of all the houses in the parish of Killsallagh? We never done wrong to no one. Did we? *(Sits Right of table Left.)* A man at my age shouldn't be worried to death. It's peace and quiet I should be having and long days by the fire.

PATRICK. But the priests must have a say in everything. If you stand up to them they call you a troublemaker and threaten the devil's horns on you with their Latin ramesh. Nora was right about them in her ravings—if it's raving she was at all.

MARY. Son, for my sake, be quiet and let the priest do his work in peace.

PATRICK. I don't believe in religion any longer or whipping or browbeating. We've stood for that kind of thing too long. It's time we were men and took the matter into our own hands. Are you coming with me or must I go alone?

MARY. Patrick, for my sake— What are you going to do?

(PATRICK *goes to the bedroom door.* MICHAEL MARTIN *follows. They stand looking off.)*

PRIEST. *(In a loud voice off.)* Adjuro te, serpens antique, per judicem vivorum et mortuorum, per factorem mundi, per eum qui habet potestatem mittendi te in gehennam ut ab hoc—

PATRICK. They have tied her to the bed like a beast. They're killing her—my sister—

PRIEST. *(Off.)* Adjuro te. Adjuro te.

(PATRICK *runs to cabinet and takes a heavy, wooden pounder and rushes to the bedroom door.* MARY KATE *intercepts him and stands with her back to the door.)*

MARY. I'll not let you in. You don't know what you're doing. You're out of your mind.

(There is a demoniacal laugh from NORA. MARY KATE,

MICHAEL MARTIN *and* PATRICK *draw back from the
door in alarm.* NORA *rushes into the kitchen with a
burst rope around her body and arms. Her dress is
torn. In one hand she carries a torn surplice and stole;
in the other, the* PRIEST'S *bag, a crucifix and candle-
sticks.* ANTHONY *rushes in after her but stands apart,
aghast.)*

NORA. *(As she rushes in.)* We've conquered him. We've
beaten him, body and soul. *(Standing with arms outstretched)* We've beaten God and the Trinity and all the
Archangels in heaven. *(She hurls the things she carries into
the fire. The flames rise and she is lit with their flickering
fire. Facing the fire, she continues.)* The Legion is here.
We'll rule the world. And soon we'll rule Him and throw
Him down from on high. *(She looks about her, runs to the
cabinet, takes from it a heap of holy pictures and hurls
them into the fire.)*

(The flames burn brighter. MARY KATE *crouches, face
downward, on the bed.* MICHAEL MARTIN *and* PAT-
RICK *stand terrified, their backs to the wall.* MARY
KATE *jumps up and rushes in terror to the bedroom
door.)*

MARY. Father! Father O'Malley! Come quick. Don't
leave us alone with her.

*(NORA *runs to the cabinet and, with her back to it, faces
the door of the bedroom. She tears the bonds from
her wrists. She is like a wild beast.* MARY KATE *draws
back from the door as* FATHER O'MALLEY *enters.
Supported by the* DOCTOR, *he stumbles in. He is now
an old, broken man, exhausted by his terrible ordeal.
He hands the* DOCTOR *aside and leans bent, against
the table, watching* NORA *like a dying man. The*
NUNS *stand in the bedroom door.)*

NORA. Look at him now! What do you think of your

holy priest and his prayers and religion? Who is the stronger now? *(She runs across and spits twice in the face of the* PRIEST. *As she spits in his face,* FATHER O'MALLEY, *by a tremendous effort of will, brings strength into his weakened frame, rises aloft and, with one hand on high, towers above the girl. As he speaks the final words of exorcism,* NORA, *unable to fight against this new power, flees crouchingly to the table, the chair, the fireplace and finally throws herself writhing in front of him on the floor. Against a jabbering background of devil voices one voice issues from her more clearly than the others saying:)* I will not leave. I will not leave.

PRIEST. Exorciso te, immundissime spiritus, omne plantasma, omnis legio, in nomine Domini nostri, Jeu Christi, eradicare et effugarte ab hoc plasmate Dei. Ipse tibi imperat, qui de te supernis caelorum in inferiora terrae demergi praecepit. In nomine Patris et Filii et Spiritus Sancti. *(He makes the sign of the cross in the air and remains standing.)*

> *(There is a moment of silence.* NORA *lies still. There is a sudden, loud jabbering from the voices.* NORA *turns face upwards, gives a shriek and stiffens. Then her head falls to one side and her body goes limp. Of a sudden it grows darker. An evil influence fills the kitchen. There is a loud jabbering.* MARY KATE *throws herself on the bed. The* OTHERS *shrink away in terror or stand flattened against the walls. The* NUNS *prostrate themselves on the floor. There is another moment of silence. Then a weaker jabbering comes from outside the house. It turns into a wail. As the wail dies away,* ANTHONY *moves to the Center door and looks out. RAIN falls suddenly. Then the light brightens and the rain stops. ALL look up and concentrate on the door. There is a little cry from* NORA. ANTHONY *comes forward quickly to her. Her eyes open and her head lifts a little.* ANTHONY *goes down on his knee beside her and supports her head.)*

Te Deum, laudamus.

ANTHONY. Nora!

(The LIGHT grows brighter. ANTHONY and PATRICK carry NORA to the bed.)

NORA. —Anthony! *(As if awakening from sleep)* Like a soft, warm wind in April— I'm at peace. I'll be troubled no more. I dreamt there was a storm. Then the storm blew over and I heard the rain. It was coming heavily on the flags in the yard and spitting through the chimney—on the fire in the hearth.

ANTHONY. Yes, the rain came down. 'Twill clear the heaviness from the air.

DOCTOR. *(Feels her pulse, puts his hand to her forehead and looks closely at her.)* Any pain—or anything?

NORA. Nothing, Doctor. I've no pain at all. I'm grand.

DOCTOR. *(Pulls up her sleeve and looks at her arm.)* They're gone! I can't understand it. *(The DOCTOR moves away.)*

MARY. *(Runs to NORA and kneels to embrace her.)* Tell me you're well. Tell me the evil has left you. My heart is sick with fret.

NORA. *(Rising and supported by her mother)* Mother! It's all over.

MARY. *(Embracing NORA)* Oh, may God be praised and His holy mother! Father, she's well. She's well. Look, Nora, himself and Patrick! They were near driven astray with the worry of it all.

(PATRICK *and* MICHAEL MARTIN *come forward.*)

NORA. Don't cry, Da. Why in the world should you be crying now?

PATRICK. *(Tenderly.)* Nora—

NORA. Poor Patseen!

PATRICK. *(Crosses to the* PRIEST.) Father, I beg your forgiveness.

PRIEST. *(Weakly.)* God will forgive you, my son.

NORA. Father, forgive me—

(ANTHONY *takes* NORA *by the hand and they move to*

the Center door and off. Exit PATRICK *with* NORA'S *shawl. Exit the* NUNS *to the bedroom. Exit* MARY KATE *and* MICHAEL MARTIN *to the bedroom. The* DOCTOR *stands looking in the fire. The* PRIEST *who has been standing erect is shaken by a sudden spasm. He looks up towards heaven. His lips mutter "Father, into Thy hands I commend my spirit." He collapses quietly on to the floor. The* DOCTOR *turns and moves quickly to him, feels his pulse and blesses himself. The* PRIEST *is dead.)*

CURTAIN

END OF PLAY

THE RIGHTEOUS ARE BOLD

PROPERTY PLOT

ACT ONE

Twig broom D.S.L.
Water bucket w/water & dipper D.L.
Egg basket w/2 eggs on hearth D.L.
Bellows hanging D.L. on fireplace
Rosary hanging D.L. on fireplace
Oil lantern D.L. on mantel
Clay pipe w/tobacco upstage of lantern
Pr. eyeglasses (Michael) U.S. of pipe
Can of tea w/spoon C. mantel
Candle in black holder C.S. of tea can
Alarm clock
Brown glass jar w/coins inside
Black glass w/3 or 4 tapers
Kerosene lamp w/candle wick
Box of kitchen matches
Rosary hanging U.S. from mantel
Pair firetongs U.S. on hearth
Can, black, with water U.S. on hearth
Round iron pot w/water on U.S. fireplace hook, spoon
    in it
Oval iron pot w/o water on D.S. fireplace hook
Brown clay teapot U.S. on fireplace hob
Clothesline hanging from D.S. to U.S. below mantel
Painting of Virgin over mantel
Wooden bench on marks D.L. front of fireplace
Wooden stool on marks U.S. of fireplace
Mirror, soaped, hanging on wall U.S. of fireplace
Table L.C. w/3 chairs at L., C. & R. On table: 3 plates,
    4 coffee cups, egg cup, 3 spoons, creamer, sugar bowl
    w/o top, bread plate

Wooden rake hanging over bed U.L.S.

Shelf over bed. On it, from S.L. to S.R.: cardboard box, pr. shoes, old suitcase

Patchwork quilt on bed

Crucifix on wall over bed

Panel in wall over bed in "Down" position (wind effect)

Shelf on wall S.R. of bed. On shelf: statue of Virgin (scored for easy breakage), red votive light

Holy water font on wall beneath shelf

Walking canes hanging S.L. of C. door on peg; black cane to the outside

Sacred Heart painting hanging over C. door

Pile of turf on shelf S.L. outside C. door

Tin pail half full of water on floor S.L. outside C. door

Suitcase w/two dresses S.L. on floor outside C. door

Coil of lash line hanging on nail S.R. outside C. door

Black shawl hanging on S.R. peg of C. door

Square table anchored to floor beneath U.R.C. window

Fake bar of soap on table

Dishpan on table

Pair work shoes under table

Harness hanging from ceiling beam D.S. of window

Dish rag hanging U.S. on cabinet

Wooden three-shelf cabinet against R. wall

On top of cabinet (checking from D.S. to U.S.): brown bowl, white tea mug, 2 cream-colored cans

On top shelf: 2 egg cups, 3 coffee mugs, tan bowl

On middle shelf: salt cellar, coffee mug, opened letter, pitcher w/milk

On first shelf: enamel pot w/paring knife and 3 potatoes, 2 mugs, plates

On top of the bottom half of the cabinet: round tin bowl, bread board on which is loaf of bread, and onstage of bread is plate w/4 slices of bread; saw edge slicing knife; sack of grain; bowl w/butter; table knife across butter bowl; wooden pounder standing

On top shelf inside cabinet are two tin basins (empty)

On bottom shelf inside cabinet is one sack containing meal

Rock hanging from roof D.R.

Rock hanging from roof against R. wall outside of house

OFF R. PROPS:

Postman's bag. Int it: medicine, dyes, pins, unopened
letter (Wilile)

Bottle of rum (Willie)

Small feather (Willie—Act III)

Piece yellow material (Willie—Act I)

Piece lace (Willie—Act I)

Piece blue material (Willie—Act I)

Shoebox in black bag. In it: 3 small tied bags & goose
quill (Willie—Act III)

Three-pronged stick (Willie—Act III)

Prayer book (Father—Act III)

Black bag (Father—Act III). In it: surplice, stole, candlestick, candle, matches, crucifix

Black bag (Doctor—Act II). In it: stethoscope, pills,
small bottle w/white medicine, etc.

Agnus Dei ((Sr. Mary—Act III)

OFF L. PROPS:

Torn surplice (Nora—Act III)

Red stole (Nora—Act III)

3 pieces white rope (Nora—Act III)

PERSONAL PROPS:

Nora: Purse containing comb and compact w/powder
and puff

Patrick: Cigarette butt

Anthony: Cigarettes and matches

ACT TWO

(After "places": Center door closed, bedroom door closed,
candle re-lit)

CLEAR:

All cups, etc., from table

Cap & scarf from mantel (Michael)

Coat, hat & gloves (Nora)

Burnt tapers
Small broken pieces of statue
Sweep S.L. area
Blow out candle
Sharp slicing knife to inside cabinet
Milk pitcher from cabinet
Bagpipes from window R.
Tin dishpan from R. table to between cabinet and R. wall

SET:

Wooden bench on Act II marks. On it: girl's sweater &
    stockings
Hang U.S. Rosary with D.S. Rosary D.L. from mantel
Wooden stool on marks. On it: Opened suitcase w/purse
    inside and on D.S. end of suitcase; 2 dresses inside
    suitcase
Table on L.C. marks
Wooden chair L. of table and facing D.S.; Right front
    leg of chair is 4 inches L. of the U.L. leg of table
Several pieces of broken statue under table and also beside
    stool
Coil of lashline on peg on U.R.C. wall
Wooden chairs on marks R.C.
Black cane to inside of 3 canes on peg L. of C. door
Girl's felt shoes C. front of bed on floor
Candle in black holder on mantel
Dull slicing knife D.S. on cabinet. Handle onstage

PERSONAL PROPS:

Doctor: Lighter, flashlight, fountain pen, prescription pad,
    pocket watch, pipe

ACT THREE

CLEAR:
Burnt tapers
Stool
Holy pictures
Crucifix

Holy water font
Shoes and purse (Nora)
Sweater and stockings (Nora)
Bottle of rum
Broken pieces of statue from fireplace

SET:
Cane bottom chair on marks D.L. facing upstage
Bench to Act III marks
Water in kettle on hob
Tin pail on floor U.R. by table
Dishpan on U.R. table
Coil of lashline on peg U.C. wall
Table on marks R.C. Chairs L., C. & R. at table (check
    that C. chair is completely under table)
On table: 2 plates, 3 cups, teapot, 2 sets cutlery, cream
    pitcher
On top of bottom half of cabinet: tin basin, bread board
    w/bread, wooden pounder (grain in basin)
Outside C. door: large wash pan set against rocks U.R.
    to catch water when thrown

PERSONAL PROPS:
Rosaries for Nuns
St. Benedict medal (Mother Benedict)

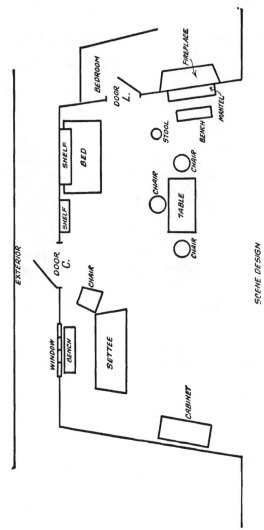

SCENE DESIGN

"THE RIGHTEOUS ARE BOLD"

OTHER TITLES AVAILABLE FROM SAMUEL FRENCH

TAKE HER, SHE'S MINE
Phoebe and Henry Ephron

Comedy / 11m, 6f / Various Sets

Art Carney and Phyllis Thaxter played the Broadway roles of parents of two typical American girls enroute to college. The story is based on the wild and wooly experiences the authors had with their daughters, Nora Ephron and Delia Ephron, themselves now well known writers. The phases of a girl's life are cause for enjoyment except to fearful fathers. Through the first two years, the authors tell us, college girls are frightfully sophisticated about all departments of human life. Then they pass into the "liberal" period of causes and humanitarianism, and some into the intellectual lethargy of beatniksville. Finally, they start to think seriously of their lives as grown ups. It's an experience in growing up, as much for the parents as for the girls.

"A warming comedy. A delightful play about parents vs kids. It's loaded with laughs. It's going to be a smash hit."
— *New York Mirror*

MURDER AMONG FRIENDS
Bob Barry

Comedy Thriller / 4m, 2f / Interior

Take an aging, exceedingly vain actor; his very rich wife; a double dealing, double loving agent, plunk them down in an elegant New York duplex and add dialogue crackling with wit and laughs, and you have the basic elements for an evening of pure, sophisticated entertainment. Angela, the wife and Ted, the agent, are lovers and plan to murder Palmer, the actor, during a contrived robbery on New Year's Eve. But actor and agent are also lovers and have an identical plan to do in the wife. A murder occurs, but not one of the planned ones.

"Clever, amusing, and very surprising."
– *New York Times*

"A slick, sophisticated show that is modern and very funny."
– WABC TV

9 780573 614781